At the Altar of the World

The Pontificate of Pope John Paul II through the Lens of L'Osservatore Romano and the Words of Ecclesia de Eucharistia

AT THE ALTAR OF THE WORLD

The Pontificate of Pope John Paul II through the Lens of L'Osservatore Romano and the Words of Ecclesia de Eucharistia

POPE JOHN PAUL II CULTURAL CENTER

CONTENTS

CREDITS

Pope John Paul II Cultural Center
Washington, DC
AT THE ALTAR OF THE WORLD
*The Pontificate of Pope John Paul II through
the Lens of L'Osservatore Romano and the Words
of Ecclesia de Eucharistia*

This book is inspired by the year-long series
of four photographic exhibitions,
AT THE ALTAR OF THE WORLD: *The Pontificate of
Pope John Paul II through the Lens of L'Osservatore
Romano and the Words of Ecclesia de Eucharistia*
at the Museums at the Pope John Paul II
Cultural Center, Washington, DC
September 10, 2003 through November 7, 2004

Reverend G. Michael Bugarin, STL, JCL
Executive Director
Pope John Paul II Cultural Center

Penelope C. Fletcher
Deputy Director/Chief Operating Officer
Pope John Paul II Cultural Center

Daniel G. Callahan
Director of Publications and Programs
Pope John Paul II Cultural Center

PHOTOGRAPHY:

All photography © L'Osservatore Romano
Mario Agnes, Editor-in-Chief

Director General
Servizio Fotografico de L'Osservatore Romano
00120 Vatican City
Don Giorgio Bruni, SDB

Additional photography:
Page 103: CNS
Page 196: Robert Burgess
Inside back cover: G. Michael Bugarin

CONTENT:

Ecclesia de Eucharistia
Text from Liberia Editrice Vaticana
Vatican City

English translation of the Rite of Dedication of an Altar
© United States Conference of Catholic Bishops

Editor: Daniel G. Callahan
Contributors: Michael J. Bransfield,
J. Augustine Di Noia, Avery Dulles, Francis George,
John J. Myers, Richard Schenk, Kenneth L. Schmitz,
Donald W. Wuerl

DESIGN:

Smarteam Communications Inc.
Gary A. Ridley, Creative Director
Polina Pinchevsky, Book Design
Mary Argodale, Book Production

PRINTING:

Printed in Italy by Bolis Poligrafiche SpA
Prepress by S&S Graphics

Library of Congress Control Number
2003111094

ISBN 0-9712981-1-4 (Hard Cover)
ISBN 0-9712981-2-2 (Soft Cover)

FOREWORD

Adam Cardinal Maida

"The Church draws her life from the Eucharist." So writes Pope John Paul II in the opening words of his fourteenth and most recent encyclical, *Ecclesia de Eucharistia.* Thanks to a close and supportive collaboration between *L'Osservatore Romano* and the Pope John Paul II Cultural Center, we have this collection of stirring photographs which bring to life our Holy Father's message on this great mystery of our faith. As you turn the pages of this book, you will discover that, like the Church itself, our Holy Father finds the source and strength for his special vocation from the same great mystery of the Holy Eucharist.

As the Church, and indeed, the world, celebrate with joy and gratitude his Silver Jubilee as Vicar of Christ and Vicar of St. Peter, quite appropriately we can focus on the Holy Eucharist as the lens through which we can meditate on his pontificate. For twenty-five years we have heard our Holy Father teach and inspire us to love Christ present in this Sacrament; *Ecclesia de Eucharistia* is the culmination of twenty-five years of the Holy Father's loving instruction on this central mystery of our faith. These rarely-seen photographs give testimony to the role of the Holy Eucharist in the life of Pope John Paul II.

In his encyclical, our Holy Father goes to great lengths to proclaim Jesus' great love for us as manifest in the Holy Eucharist: "I want once more to recall this truth and to join you, my dear brothers and sisters, in adoration before this mystery: a great mystery, a mystery of mercy. What more could Jesus have done for us? Truly in the Eucharist, he shows us a love which goes 'to the end' (cf. *Jn* 13:1), a love which knows no measure." Concurrent with these words, *L'Osservatore Romano* photographs illustrate the Holy Father's love for Jesus and for all of us *to the end.* As he has said, "It is wonderful to be able to give oneself to the very end for the sake of the kingdom of God" (*Letter to the Elderly [1999]*).

Who could have predicted the astounding quarter-century that lay ahead of him when the world first caught sight of our new pope that autumn evening of October 16, 1978? Man of God and Son of Poland, Pope John Paul II filled the shoes of the Fisherman and won our hearts. For the past twenty-five remarkable years, his pace has been unrelenting: he has seen and been seen by more people, met with more world leaders and visited more countries than any of his predecessors. An instrumental part in the fall of Communism in Eastern Europe and a national hero in Poland for his support of the Solidarity movement, the Holy Father has been a tireless champion and voice for human rights and human life and the dignity of humankind. He has built bridges between nations, cultures and religious traditions. With endless courage and zeal, he proclaimed the Good News to all who were willing to listen.

The beautiful photography contained herein captures in some small but significant way our Holy Father's legacy. Page by page, these images conjure memories, stir faith and inspire love for Pope John Paul II and for the God who lovingly gave him to us. As we all know, the perfect response to a gift is gratitude. This book inspired by the Eucharist, *thanksgiving,* is then the perfect response for so great a legacy. 🍇

ADAM CARDINAL MAIDA is Archbishop of Detroit and President of the Pope John Paul II Cultural Center. His vision led to the founding of the Cultural Center.

REMARKS

BY THE PRESIDENT OF THE UNITED STATES OF AMERICA
AT THE OPENING OF THE POPE JOHN PAUL II CULTURAL CENTER

George W. Bush

… When Cardinal Wojtyla spoke here at Catholic University in 1976, few imagined the course his life would take, or the history his life would shape. In 1978, most of the world knew him only as the Polish Pope. There were signs of something different and deeper.

One journalist, after hearing the new Pope's first blessing in St. Peter's Square wired back to his editors: "This is not a pope from Poland, this is a pope from Galilee." From that day to this, the Pope's life has written one of the great inspiring stories of our time.

We remember the Pope's first visit to Poland in 1979 when faith turned into resistance and began the swift collapse of imperial communism. The gentle, young priest, once ordered into forced labor by Nazis, became the foe of tyranny and a witness to hope.

The last leader of the Soviet Union would call him "the highest moral authority on earth." We remember his visit to a prison, comforting the man who shot him. By answering violence with forgiveness, the Pope became a symbol of reconciliation.

We remember the Pope's visit to Manila in 1995, speaking to one of the largest crowds in history, more than five-million men and women and children. We remember that as a priest fifty years ago, he traveled by horse-cart to teach the children of small villages. Now he's kissed the ground of 123 countries and leads a flock of one billion into the Third Millennium.

We remember the Pope's visit to Israel and his mission of reconciliation and mutual respect between Christians and Jews. He is the first modern pope to enter a synagogue or visit an Islamic country. He has always combined the practice of tolerance with a passion for truth.

John Paul, himself, has often said, "In the designs of Providence, there are no mere coincidences," and maybe the reason this man became Pope is that he bears the message our world needs to hear. To the poor, sick and dying, he carries a message of dignity and solidarity with their suffering. Even when they are forgotten by man, he reminds them they are never forgotten by God.

"Do not give in to despair," he said in the South Bronx. "God has your lives and his care goes with you, calls you to better things, calls you to overcome."

To the wealthy, this Pope carries the message that wealth alone is a false comfort. The goods of the world, he teaches, are nothing without goodness. We are called, each and every one of us, not only to make our own way, but to ease the path of others.

To those with power, the Pope carries a message of justice and human rights. And that message has caused dictators to fear and to fall. His is not the power of armies or technology or wealth. It is the unexpected power of a baby in a stable, of a man on a cross, of a simple fisherman who carried a message of hope to Rome.

Pope John Paul II brings that message of liberation to every corner of the world. When he arrived in Cuba in 1998, he was greeted by signs that read, "Fidel is the Revolution!" But as the Pope's biographer put it, "In the next four days Cuba belonged to another revolutionary." We are confident that the revolution of hope the Pope began in that nation will bear fruit in our time.

And we're responsible to stand for human dignity and religious freedom wherever they are denied, from Cuba to China to Southern Sudan. And we, in our country, must not ignore the words the Pope addresses to us. On his four pilgrimages to America, he has spoken with wisdom and feeling about our strengths and our flaws, our successes and our needs.

The Pope reminds us that, while freedom defines our nation, responsibility must define our lives. He challenges us to live up to our aspirations, to be a fair and just society where all are welcomed, all are valued and all are protected. And he is never more eloquent than when he speaks for a culture of life. The culture of life is a welcoming culture, never excluding, never dividing, never despairing and always affirming the goodness of life in all its seasons.

In the culture of life, we must make room for the stranger. We must comfort the sick. We must care for the aged. We must welcome the immigrant. We must teach our children to be gentle with one another. We must defend in love the innocent child waiting to be born.

The center we dedicate today celebrates the Pope's message, its comfort and its challenge. This place stands for the dignity of the human person, the value of every life and the splendor of truth. And above all it stands, in the Pope's words, for the "joy of faith in a troubled world."

I'm grateful that Pope John Paul II chose Washington as the site for this Center. It brings honor and it fills a need. We are thankful for the message. We are also thankful for the messenger, for his personal warmth and prophetic strength; for his good humor and his bracing honesty; for his spiritual and intellectual gifts; for his moral courage, tested against tyranny and against our own complacency.

Always, the Pope points us to the things that last and the love that saves. We thank God for this rare man, a servant of God and a hero of history. And I thank all of you for building this center of conscience and reflection in our Nation's Capital.

GOD BLESS.

GEORGE W. BUSH, forty-third President of the United States, delivered this speech at the opening of the Pope John Paul II Cultural Center on March 22, 2001.

INTRODUCTION

Reverend G. Michael Bugarin

We started with a simple idea: a photography exhibition presented at the Pope John Paul II Cultural Center that would showcase the pontificate of Pope John Paul II to mark the Silver Jubilee Year in his extraordinary papacy. In March and April of this year, I was part of a team of Cultural Center staff who were privileged to have access to the photo archives of the Vatican's official newspaper, *L'Osservatore Romano*. Behind the service desks at the *Servizio Fotografico* in Vatican City, where pilgrims and tourists queue in line to purchase photographs taken by the Vatican photographers at public Masses and general audiences, is an archival storage room. That room is lined floor to ceiling with rows and rows of open shelving, which are in turn lined back to back with photo storage boxes arranged in chronological order by date. At the very far end of the room is the original box, marked "1" — 16 Ottobre 1978, the date of the election of Pope John Paul II to the papacy.

The boxes proceed in numerical order and the years accumulate across the shelving down the room until the numbers reach well over 2,900. The photographs in these nearly three thousand boxes represent only the Holy Father's time in Rome and Italy; the Apostolic Journeys to over 125 countries are kept separately and have a numbering system all their own. In April 2003 there was less than one shelving unit still available for storage. In the nearly six months which have passed since our stay there, I can only imagine the *Servizio Fotografico* has had to rearrange the furniture.

A discovery in the early stages of our research made it clear how remarkable these numbers truly are. Separated from the other archive boxes on the empty shelving were three boxes; two were marked "Paolo VI" and one "Giovanni Paolo I." Keeping in mind that Pope Paul VI had a fifteen-year pontificate, the quantity of photographs taken during the pontificate of Pope John Paul II is staggering.

The quantity impressed us at first, but ultimately, it was the quality of the photography that overwhelmed us. The pictures we were seeing in these dusty boxes were something much different than the photography you would expect to be seen in *Time* or *Newsweek*. With each opened box a unique portrait of the Holy Father was emerging, that has not been readily available in the everyday press. The camera lenses at *L'Osservatore Romano* have succeeded in capturing the deeply spiritual essence of Pope John Paul II.

Having collected nearly two thousand images and with many archival boxes still unopened, we returned to the Cultural Center. While we were pondering how we should present the photographs thematically, the Holy Father issued to great acclaim his fourteenth encyclical *Ecclesia de Eucharistia*. The personal sentiment and heartfelt devotion which flowed from this encyclical on the Eucharist in its relationship to the Church inspired us to format the photography around the words of this beautiful document. Stunningly beautiful photographs suddenly become, in the context of the encyclical, breathtaking and exquisite storytelling. The juxtaposition of the image and the word present a complete and compelling story of the Pope's pontificate in a truly unique and significant way. At the same time, the Holy Father's teaching on the Holy Eucharist is made even more accessible. The result of this collaboration between images and words is *At the Altar of the World: The Pontificate of Pope John Paul II through the Lens of L'Osservatore Romano and the Words of Ecclesia de Eucharistia.*

The simple idea of a photography exhibition to celebrate the Silver Jubilee Year in the Pontificate of Pope John Paul II had evolved into something unique and much more significant—an idea so compelling that the idea of this book took root.

In his encyclical, Pope John Paul II refers to the cosmic character of the Eucharist: "I have been able to celebrate Holy Mass in chapels built along mountain paths, on lakeshores and seacoasts; I have celebrated it on altars built in stadiums and in city squares. ...This varied scenario of celebrations of the Eucharist has given me a powerful experience of its universal and, so to speak, cosmic character. Yes, cosmic! Because even when it is celebrated on the humble altar of a country church, the Eucharist is always in some way celebrated *on the altar of the world*. It unites heaven and earth. It embraces and permeates all creation (*Ecclesia de Eucharistia, 8*)."

While the Eucharist is celebrated on *the altar of the world*, this book honors Pope John Paul II and his extraordinary 25 years of ministry of celebrating the Eucharist *at the altar of the world* as Bishop of Rome and shepherd of the universal Church on earth. The photographs herein are placed with excerpts from the encyclical to give a clear understanding of Pope John Paul II's commitment, devotion and dedication to Christ Present in the Holy Eucharist. Additionally, eight prominent Church leaders and scholars have contributed essays elaborating on the encyclical and the Holy Father's pontificate in the context of his beautiful teaching on the Most Blessed Sacrament.

There are many people to acknowledge for their help with this volume. Our work would not have been possible without the cooperation and support of the photographers themselves, Don Giorgio Bruni, Arturo Mari and Francesco Sforza. They helped with our work in Italy, but they also inspired us with their life's work. They and the staff at *L'Osservatore Romano* made a daunting task possible. Many thanks go also to the Cultural Center staff for their work and devotion. Daniel G. Callahan, Director of Publications, ably edited the words and photographs, crafting each page as a beautiful tribute. Penelope C. Fletcher, Deputy Director and our curator, Rebecca Phillips Abbott, gave many hours to the project as it grew in scope and meaning. The assistance of Gary Ridley and Polina Pinchevsky of Smarteam Communications during the design phase of the project was also invaluable. All involved with the project brought to it a love for Pope John Paul II that gave inspiration and unity to this project.

Pope John Paul has clearly lived the words he teaches through this encyclical. "Every commitment to holiness, every activity aimed at carrying out the Church's mission, every work of pastoral planning," he writes, "must draw the strength it needs from the Eucharistic mystery and in turn be directed to that mystery." These photographs clearly demonstrate the Holy Father's commitment to these words. In the same way, this book demonstrates the Pope John Paul II Cultural Center's commitment to what the Pope calls the "New Evangelization." Following the Holy Father's example and teachings, the Cultural Center strives to fulfill its mission of proclaiming the Good News through our unique museum experience and educational and catechetical programs. This book is yet another opportunity in which the Pope John Paul II Cultural Center can move beyond its physical walls to accomplish this mission. Inspired by the Holy Father's words in *Ecclesia de Eucharistia*, we pray to obtain our strength from the Eucharistic mystery and in turn dedicate our work to it. 🐝

REVEREND G. MICHAEL BUGARIN is the Executive Director of the Pope John Paul II Cultural Center.

THE CHURCH DRAWS HER LIFE FROM THE EUCHARIST

Most Reverend Donald W. Wuerl, STD

On Holy Thursday, April 17, 2003, our Holy Father, Pope John Paul II, issued the encyclical letter, *Ecclesia de Eucharistia: On the Eucharist in its Relationship to the Church*. In the introduction, he tells us why he chose this particular moment and how it is part of a much larger tradition going back to the very beginning of his pontificate. "From the time I began my ministry as the Successor of Peter, I have always marked Holy Thursday, the day of the Eucharist and of the priesthood, by sending a letter to all of the priests of the world. This year, the twenty-fifth of my pontificate, I wish to involve the whole Church more fully in this eucharistic reflection, also as a way of thanking the Lord for the gift of the Eucharist and the priesthood: Gift and Mystery" (*Ecclesia de Eucharistia* 7).

THE CHURCH DRAWS HER LIFE FROM THE EUCHARIST

As he begins the encyclical, the Holy Father articulates concisely the theme he will develop throughout the whole text: "The Church draws her life from the Eucharist" (*EdE* 1). Here he is speaking not just about the regular experience of faith that all of us know from our own participation in daily, and particularly, Sunday eucharistic liturgy but more importantly about the very heart of the mystery of the Church.

Jesus intends to remain with us; freely he offers himself on the cross for our salvation. His death and resurrection ransomed us from sin and introduced us into the new life of adopted sonship with God. How would this sacred, saving action continue generation after generation, age after age? How would each successive generation have access to the grace of salvation?

Jesus fulfills his promise to be with us to the very end of time in the Holy Eucharist. In the changing of bread and wine into the body and blood of the Lord, the Church rejoices in Christ's presence with unique intensity. "Ever since Pentecost, when the Church, the People of the New Covenant, began her pilgrim journey toward her heavenly homeland, the Divine Sacrament has continued to mark the passing of her days, filling them with confident hope" (*EdE* 1). This theme is continually touched upon by the Holy Father and he develops it in successive chapters.

Most Reverend Donald W. Wuerl is Bishop of Pittsburgh and Vice-President of the Pope John Paul II Cultural Center charged with oversight of the Intercultural Forum for Studies in Faith and Culture. He is nationally known from the television program, *The Teaching of Christ*; his best-selling adult catechism of the same name is in its 27th year of publication.

FAITH'S GREAT MYSTERY

In Chapter One, "The Mystery of Faith," we are reminded by the Pope that it was Jesus who instituted the Eucharist, which is the memorial of the Lord's death and resurrection, and that each time the Church celebrates the eucharistic liturgy, the central event of our salvation becomes sacramentally but really present (cf. *EdE* 11, 15). In meditating on the Mystery of Faith, the Holy Father reminds us that it is Christ who is at the very core of the sacraments and, particularly, the Eucharist. Jesus continues to act through the sacraments; it is the Lord who is present in every one of the seven sacraments, thus producing the spiritual effect that the outward sign demonstrates. The Pope recalls for us that "the sacramental re-presentation of Christ's sacrifice, crowned by the resurrection, in the Mass involves a most special presence which—in the words of Paul VI—is called real not as a way of excluding all other types of presence as if they were not real, but because it is a presence in the fullest sense: a substantial presence whereby Christ, the God-man, is wholly and entirely present" (*EdE* 15).

In a strikingly personal reference, our Holy Father recounts how during the Great Jubilee of the year 2000 he had the "opportunity to celebrate the Eucharist in the Cenacle of Jerusalem where, according to tradition, it was first celebrated by Jesus himself. The Upper Room was where this most Holy Sacrament was instituted. It is there that Jesus took bread, broke it and gave it to his disciples saying, 'Take this all of you and eat it: this is my body which will be given up for you' (cf. *Mt* 26:26; *Lk* 22:19; *1 Cor* 11:24). Then he took the cup of wine and said to them: 'Take this all of you and drink from it. This is the cup of my blood, the blood of the new and everlasting covenant. It will be shed for you and for all, so that sins may be forgiven' (cf. *Mk* 14:24; *Lk* 22:20; *1 Cor* 11:25)" (*EdE* 2). The Pope goes on to share with us, "I am grateful to the Lord Jesus for allowing me to repeat in that same place, in obedience to his command: 'Do this in remembrance of me' (*Lk* 22:19), the words which he spoke two thousand years ago" (*EdE* 2).

The origins of the Eucharist are found in the Last Supper. In order to leave us a pledge of his love and never depart from us, but rather to make us sharers in his Passover, Jesus instituted the Eucharist as the memorial of his death and resurrection and commanded the Apostles to celebrate it until he returned. In the Last Supper, Jesus instituted the new memorial sacrifice. The true Lamb of God (*Jn* 1:29) was about to be slain. By his cross and resurrection he was to free not just one nation from the bondage of human slavery but all humanity from the more bitter slavery of sin.

There is only one sacrifice—the self-giving of Christ on the cross at Calvary. Again our Holy Father highlights this reality. Once and for all, Jesus, who was the victim for our sins, offered himself up for our salvation. As the letter to the Hebrews affirms: "For this reason he is mediator of a new covenant: since a death has taken place for deliverance from the transgressions under the first covenant, those who are called may receive the promised eternal inheritance" (*Heb* 9:15).

The one great sacrifice was accomplished by Jesus the Priest and Victim who offered himself on the altar of the cross for our redemption. This sacrifice not only need not—it cannot—be repeated. However, it can be re-presented so that we today, in our moment in history, are able sacramentally and spiritually to enter the paschal mystery and draw spiritual nourishment from it. Our Holy Father returns over and over again to this theme throughout each chapter of *Ecclesia de Eucharistia*.

THE KINGDOM OF GOD IN OUR MIDST

In the second chapter, entitled "The Eucharist Builds the Church," our Holy Father recalls for us that the Eucharist is at the center of the process of the Church's growth. The Church's life and development are rooted in the sacrifice of the cross, which is re-represented on the altar (cf. *EdE* 21). In beginning this chapter, the Pope turns to the Second Vatican Council's teaching. Quoting the Dogmatic Constitution on the Church, *Lumen Gentium*, the Holy Father points out that "the Church, as the Kingdom of Christ already present in mystery, grows visibly in the world through the power of God" (*EdE* 21). As if in answer to the question: "How does the

Church grow?" the Pope cites the Council: "as often as the sacrifice of the cross by which 'Christ our paschal lamb is sacrificed' (*1 Cor* 5: 7) is celebrated on the altar, the work of our redemption is carried out. At the same time in the sacrament of the eucharistic bread, the unity of the faithful, who form one body in Christ (cf. *1 Cor* 10:17), is both expressed and brought about" (*EdE* 21).

Jesus established the Eucharist in a way that would allow all of us to participate in it as his new body. We are not just individuals standing before God; we are also a community of believers, God's family, the people of God, the body of Christ. It is for this reason that "the Eucharist, which is in an outstanding way the sacrament of the paschal mystery, stands at the center of the Church's life" (*EdE* 3).

The Holy Father reminds us that in the earliest chapters of the Acts of the Apostles, which describe the life of the ancient, fledgling Church, we find the description of the faithful coming together in order that they might devote "themselves to the Apostles' teaching and the fellowship, to the breaking of bread and the prayers (*Acts* 2:42). The 'breaking of the bread' refers to the Eucharist" (*EdE* 3). Two-thousand years later, the Pope teaches us, we continue to re-live that primordial image of the Church.

The Church shares in the very life of the Risen Lord. Its members, through baptism into the Church, form a body with Christ as its head. It is through this Church that women and men are saved by coming to know Jesus Christ and through him are united in grace to the Father through the outpouring of the Holy Spirit. As the Holy Father makes clear, the mystery of the faith involves the mystery of the Eucharist and the Church.

After the celebrant holds up the consecrated host and the chalice of precious blood for the veneration of the people at Mass, he genuflects in adoration and then joins the people in a proclamation that expresses the core of our Christian faith. As the priest proclaims "the mystery of faith," all present respond as the encyclical highlights for us: "We announce your death, O Lord, and we proclaim your resurrection until you come in glory" (*EdE* 5).

By way of pastoral application, the Holy Father highlights the importance of eucharistic Communion as the "unifying power of participation in the banquet of the Eucharist" (*EdE* 23). The encyclical also reminds us that "the worship of the Eucharist outside of the Mass is of inestimable value for the life of the Church. … It is the responsibility of pastors to encourage, also by their personal witness, the practice of eucharistic adoration, and exposition of the Blessed Sacrament in particular …" (*EdE* 25).

FEED MY SHEEP

In the third chapter, entitled "The Apostolicity of the Eucharist and the Church," the Pope addresses what it means to say, first of all, that the Church is apostolic and, therefore, the Eucharist participates in that characteristic. At the core of this teaching is the recognition that the Church rests on the foundation of the Apostles. "The Eucharist too has its foundation in the Apostles, not in the sense that it did not originate in Christ himself, but because it was entrusted by Jesus to the Apostles and has been handed down to us by them and by their successors" (*EdE* 27). Another sense in which the Church is apostolic is that, with the help of the Holy Spirit, the Church hands on the deposit of faith that she received from the Apostles. The Pope points out that here too the Eucharist is apostolic, "for it is celebrated in conformity with the faith of the Apostles" (*EdE* 27).

Lastly we are told the Church is apostolic in the sense that she continues to be taught, sanctified and guided by the Apostles until Christ's return. The Eucharist "also expresses this sense of apostolicity" since it is the ordained priest who, acting in the person of Christ, brings about the eucharistic sacrifice and offers it to God in the name of all the people. The Holy Father, at this point, notes "For this reason, the Roman Missal prescribes that only the priest should recite the Eucharistic Prayer, while the people participate in faith and in silence" (*EdE* 28).

A pastoral implication for chapter three is the "pastoral promotion of priestly vocations" (*EdE* 31). We are all obliged to pray and work for an increase in priestly vocations. We are reminded that when a community lacks a priest and a remedy is sought in having religious or laity lead the faithful in prayer, as praiseworthy as this exercise is, "such solutions must be considered merely temporary, while the community awaits a priest" (*EdE* 32).

A COMMUNION OF BELIEVERS

Chapter Four is entitled "The Eucharist and Ecclesial Communion" and provides us insight into what it means to profess our faith in the Church as a "communion" of believers professing the same faith, celebrating the same sacraments and recognizing the same hierarchical structure. The Eucharist is the supreme sacramental manifestation of communion in the Church and, therefore, those who receive Holy Communion bear public witness that the outward bonds of communion are in tact (cf. *EdE* 34, 38, 40).

Underlining this truth, the Holy Father teaches: "The celebration of the Eucharist, however, cannot be the starting-point for communion; it presupposes that communion already exists, a communion which it seeks to consolidate and bring to perfection. The sacrament is an expression of this bond of communion both in its invisible dimension ... and in its visible dimension, which entails communion in the teaching of the Apostles, in the sacraments and in the Church's hierarchical order" (*EdE* 35). The encyclical goes on to remind us that we must be spiritually disposed to receive the Eucharist. "Anyone conscious of a grave sin must receive the sacrament of Reconciliation before coming to Communion" (*EdE* 36).

The reason why there cannot be intercommunion among those who do not share Catholic faith is because Communion is the public statement that those who receive it are "incorporated into the society of the Church ... accept her whole structure and all the means of salvation established within her, and within her visible framework are united to Christ, who governs her through the Supreme Pontiff and the Bishops, by the bonds of profession of faith, the sacraments and ecclesiastical government and communion" (*EdE* 38).

The fifth chapter, entitled "The Dignity of the Eucharistic Celebration," challenges us to recognize that the celebration of the Eucharist must be done with fitting simplicity and solemnity, and thus always in accord with the ritual of the Church. The Eucharist is the patrimony of the Church and not the private property of the celebrant (cf. *EdE* 47, 49, 52). The way the Eucharist is celebrated should reflect the faith and practice of the Church. "With this heightened sense of mystery, we understand how the faith of the Church in the mystery of the Eucharist has found historical expression not only in the demand for an interior disposition of devotion, but also in outward forms meant to evoke and emphasize the grandeur of the event being celebrated. This led progressively to the development of a particular form of regulating the eucharistic liturgy with due respect for the various legitimately constructed ecclesial traditions" (*EdE* 49).

MODEL OF PRAISE AND THANKSGIVING

In the final section, Chapter Six, "At the School of Mary, Woman of the Eucharist," the Pope leads us through a beautiful reflection on Mary as the model of faith and her spirit of the praise of God as a model of our own attitude as we approach the Eucharist (cf. *EdE* 54, 58). As in all of his encyclicals, the Holy Father brings forth from his own deep and beautiful devotion to Mary the Mother of Jesus, a meditation on her place in the Church and in the life of each believer. "In the Eucharist the Church is completely united to Christ and his sacrifice, and makes her own the spirit of Mary. ... The Eucharist, like the Canticle of Mary, is first and foremost praise and thanksgiving" (*EdE* 58).

The faith of the Church in the real presence of Jesus in the Eucharist goes back to the words of Jesus himself, as recorded in the Gospel of Saint John. In the eucharistic discourse after the multiplication of the loaves, our Lord contrasted ordinary bread with a bread that is not of his world but which contains eternal life for those who eat it. He said: "I am the bread of life. ... I am the living bread that came down from heaven; whoever eats of this bread will live forever and the bread that I will give is my flesh for the life of the world" (*Jn* 6:48-51).

In his masterful encyclical letter, *Ecclesia de Eucharistia*, Pope John Paul II celebrates the mystery of our faith, so beautifully proclaimed at every eucharistic liturgy, every Mass. Jesus continues to be with us. His eucharistic presence is the foundation of the Church and our pledge of life everlasting. How blessed we are with the gift of faith and, in that faith, the gift of the Eucharist.

THE CHURCH DRAWS HER LIFE FROM THE EUCHARIST.

Ecclesia de Eucharistia (1)

More than 100,000 pilgrims crowd St. Peter's Square for the Canonization Mass for Padre Pio in June, 2002.

I WILL GO TO THE ALTAR OF GOD, THE GOD OF MY JOY.
Rite of Dedication of an Altar

Top left: The Pope kisses the altar at the beginning of an outdoor Mass in Poland, 1997. Top right: The Holy Father in Detroit, 1987. Bottom: The Pope celebrates the Eucharist in the Sistine Chapel, 1980. Opposite: As a gesture of respect, the Pope kisses the ground when he arrives in a country for the first time, as he did in Spain, 1982.

During the Great Jubilee of the Year 2000,
I had an opportunity to celebrate the Eucharist in the Cenacle
of Jerusalem where, according to tradition,
it was first celebrated by Jesus himself.
The Upper Room was where this most holy Sacrament
was instituted. It is there that Christ took bread, broke it
and gave it to his disciples, saying: "Take this, all of you, and eat it:
this is my body which will be given up for you"
(cf. *Mt* 26:26; *Lk* 22:19; *1 Cor* 11:24).
Then he took the cup of wine and said to them:
"Take this, all of you and drink from it: this is the cup of my blood,
the blood of the new and everlasting covenant.
It will be shed for you and for all, so that sins may be forgiven"
(cf. *Mk* 14:24; *Lk* 22:20; *1 Cor* 11:25).
I am grateful to the Lord Jesus for allowing me to repeat
in that same place, in obedience to his command:
"Do this in memory of me" (*Lk* 22:19),
the words which he spoke two-thousand years ago.

Ecclesia de Eucharistia (1)

The Holy Father enters the Cenacle, traditional site of the "Upper Room" of the Last Supper, in Jerusalem, March 2000.
Opposite: The Pope on the Altar of the Confessio in the Patriarchal Basilica of St. Peter, Rome, 1996.

Top: His Holiness Pope John Paul II concelebrates the Eucharist with His Beatitude Lubomyr Cardinal Husar, Major Archbishop of Lviv in Ukraine, 2001. Bottom left: The Holy Father in prayer before the "Mensa Christi" in the Church of the Primacy of Peter in the Holy Land, March 2000. Bottom right: The Pope meditates at the Basilica of the Agony, on the site of the Garden of Gethsemane in the Holy Land, March, 2000.

✢

MAY THIS ALTAR BE A PLACE WHERE THE GREAT MYSTERIES OF REDEMPTION
ARE ACCOMPLISHED: A PLACE WHERE OUR PEOPLE OFFER THEIR GIFTS,
UNFOLD THEIR GIFTS, AND ECHO EVERY MEANING OF THEIR FAITH AND DEVOTION.

Concluding Prayer to the Litany of Saints, Rite of Dedication of an Altar

Consistory in the Patriarchal Basilica of St. Peter, May 2001. Next page: Pope John Paul II celebrates the Eucharist in England, 1982.

WHEN I THINK OF THE EUCHARIST, AND LOOK AT MY LIFE AS A PRIEST,
AS A BISHOP AND AS THE SUCCESSOR OF PETER,
I NATURALLY RECALL THE MANY TIMES AND PLACES IN WHICH
I WAS ABLE TO CELEBRATE IT. I REMEMBER THE PARISH CHURCH OF NIEGOWIĆ,
WHERE I HAD MY FIRST PASTORAL ASSIGNMENT,
THE COLLEGIATE CHURCH OF SAINT FLORIAN IN KRAKOW,
WAWEL CATHEDRAL, SAINT PETER'S BASILICA AND SO MANY BASILICAS
AND CHURCHES IN ROME AND THROUGHOUT THE WORLD.
I HAVE BEEN ABLE TO CELEBRATE HOLY MASS IN CHAPELS BUILT
ALONG MOUNTAIN PATHS, ON LAKESHORES AND SEACOASTS;
I HAVE CELEBRATED IT ON ALTARS BUILT IN STADIUMS AND IN CITY SQUARES ...
THIS VARIED SCENARIO OF CELEBRATIONS OF THE EUCHARIST
HAS GIVEN ME A POWERFUL EXPERIENCE OF ITS UNIVERSAL AND,
SO TO SPEAK, COSMIC CHARACTER. YES, COSMIC!
BECAUSE EVEN WHEN IT IS CELEBRATED ON THE HUMBLE ALTAR
OF A COUNTRY CHURCH, THE EUCHARIST IS ALWAYS IN SOME WAY
CELEBRATED ON THE *ALTAR OF THE WORLD*.

Ecclesia de Eucharistia (8)

The Holy Father in Rwanda, 1990. Opposite: The Pope greets a throng of people in India, 1986.

HERE IS PREPARED THE LORD'S TABLE,
AT WHICH YOUR CHILDREN NOURISHED BY THE BODY OF CHRIST,
ARE GATHERED INTO A CHURCH, ONE AND HOLY.

Preface to the Eucharistic Prayer, Rite of Dedication of an Altar

At the World's Altars. Top left: Nigeria, 1998. Top right: Poland, 1999. Bottom: United States, 1987.

Now I would like to tell you something personal.
With the passing of time, the most important and beautiful thing
for me remains the fact that I have been a priest for more
than fifty years, because every day I can celebrate Holy Mass!
The Eucharist is the secret of my day.
It gives strength and meaning to all my activities of service
to the Church and to the whole world.

Pope John Paul II, General Audience, October 8, 1997

THE MYSTERY OF FAITH

J. Augustine Di Noia, OP, STM, PhD

There is a story going around the Vatican that, when the possibility of a document on the Holy Eucharist was broached to the Holy Father, he immediately seized upon the project as his own. After addressing so many important doctrinal and moral matters in his encyclicals and other documents, Pope John Paul II said that he wanted to devote what would be his fourteenth encyclical to the theme of the mystery of the Eucharist.

So it happened that on Holy Thursday 2003, during the twenty-fifth year of a pontificate already impressive for its magisterial output, Pope John Paul II put his signature to the remarkably personal *Encyclical Letter on the Eucharist in its Relationship to the Church, Ecclesia de Eucharistia.* "I cannot let this Holy Thursday 2003 pass," he wrote, "without halting before the 'eucharistic face' of Christ and pointing out with new force to the Church the centrality of the Eucharist."

POPE JOHN PAUL II AND THE EUCHARIST

Although Pope John Paul II has never before devoted an entire encyclical to the Holy Eucharist, it is by no means the first time that he has taken up the topic. Already in his first encyclical, the programmatic *Redemptor Hominis* (1979), Pope John Paul II announced a theme that would be prominent in his later encyclical, *Ecclesia de Eucharistia,* when he wrote that it "is an essential truth, not only of doctrine but of life, that the Eucharist builds the Church, building it into the authentic community of the People of God, as the assembly of the faithful, bearing the same mark of unity that was shared by the Apostles and the first disciples of the Lord" (*Redemptor Hominis* 20).

The Holy Father has returned to the theme many times in his encyclicals and other discourses, but in order to mark another Holy Thursday early in his pontificate, he addressed to the Church a substantial apostolic letter on the Eucharist. The year was 1980 and the letter was called *Dominicae Cenae.* Like other annual Holy Thursday letters by Pope John Paul II, this one was addressed especially to bishops and priests and was devoted "to certain aspects of the eucharistic mystery and its impact on the lives of those who are ministers of it."

J. Augustine Di Noia, OP, the founding director of the Pope John Paul II Cultural Center's Intercultural Forum for Studies in Faith and Culture, is the Under-Secretary for the Congregation on the Doctrine of the Faith in Vatican City. Among his many published works is the book, *The Diversity of Religions: A Christian Perspective.*

Taking up the themes of communion, sacrifice and presence that he would address more fully in *Ecclesia de Eucharistia*, Pope John Paul II wrote in *Dominicae Cenae*, "Thanks to the council we have realized with renewed force the following truth: Just as the Church 'makes the Eucharist' so 'the Eucharist builds up' the Church. … The Church was founded, as the new community of the people of God, in the apostolic community of those Twelve who, at the Last Supper, became partakers of the body and blood of the Lord under the species of bread and wine" (*Dominicae Cenae* 4). This community is grounded, not in human fraternity as such, but in the paschal mystery: "The Church is brought into being when, in that fraternal union and communion, we celebrate the sacrifice of the cross of Christ … and we approach as a community the table of the Lord, in order to be nourished there, in a sacramental manner, by the fruits of the Holy Sacrifice of propitiation" (*DC* 4). The intimacy with us that God so much desires is achieved in a special way through this sharing in the paschal mystery and through worship of the Eucharist. In *Dominicae Cenae*, Pope John Paul II wrote: "Eucharistic worship is not so much worship of the inaccessible transcendence as the worship of the divine condescension, and it is also the merciful and redeeming transformation of the world in the human heart" (*DC* 7).

Pope John Paul II has made it one of the priorities of his pontificate to encourage and promote devotion to the eucharistic presence of Christ. *Dominicae Cenae* sounds this theme in lines that have been widely and frequently quoted: "The Church and the world have a great need for eucharistic worship. Jesus awaits us in this sacrament of love. Let us not refuse the time to meet him in adoration, in contemplation, full of faith and open to making amends for the serious offenses and crimes of the world. Let our adoration never cease" (*DC* 3). In the year following the publication of *Dominicae Cenae*, on December 2, 1981, the Holy Father inaugurated perpetual eucharistic adoration in a chapel in The Patriarchal Basilica of St. Peter. In many of his pastoral visits (notably in his discourses at Seville in 1993, Liege in 1996 and Wroclaw in 1997), Pope John Paul II has encouraged the faithful to visits to the Blessed Sacrament, exposition and adoration benediction of the Blessed Sacrament, Holy Hours and eucharistic processions. The new encyclical echoes these themes.

Ecclesia de Eucharistia: The Eucharist in its Relationship to the Church

Considered in the light of his entire ministry as the Successor of Peter, Pope John Paul's encyclical, *Ecclesia de Eucharistia*, can be seen as the culmination of twenty-five years of preaching and teaching about the Holy Eucharist. He himself invokes an even broader perspective at the start of the encyclical when he cites "the lively concern which [the Church] has always shown for the eucharistic mystery, a concern which finds authoritative expression in the work of the Councils and the Popes," in particular the Councils of Trent and Vatican II, as well as the encyclical letters of his predecessors: *Mirae Caritatis* of Leo XIII (1902), *Mediator Dei* of Pius XII (1947) and *Mysterium Fidei* of Paul VI. More immediately, the Holy Father explicitly relates the themes of the new encyclical to his own apostolic letter, *Dominicae Cenae*: "Today I take up anew the thread of that argument, with even greater emotion and gratitude in my heart …" (*Ecclesia de Eucharistia* 9).

In taking up the topic anew in 2003, Pope John Paul II notes the many positive signs of the centrality of the Eucharist in the life of the Church, in particular the active participation of the faithful in the celebration of the Sacrifice of the Mass and the renewed practices of eucharistic worship. But he also notes that, "alongside these lights, there are also shadows," among which he cites the neglect of eucharistic adoration in some places; abuses in liturgical celebration; the erosion of the sacrificial meaning of the Eucharist; confusion about the role of the ministerial priesthood in the celebration of the Eucharist and inappropriate ecumenical initiatives leading to eucharistic practices contrary to the Church's faith and discipline. "It is my hope," states the Holy Father, "that the present encyclical letter will effectively help to banish the dark clouds of unacceptable doctrine and practice, so that the Eucharist will continue to shine forth in all its radiant mystery" (*EdE* 10).

Ecclesia de Eucharistia unfolds the Church's doctrine of the Eucharist in a series of six chapters taking up in turn: the mystery of faith, the Eucharist as the source of the life of the Church, the apostolicity of the

Eucharist and of the Church, the Eucharist and ecclesial communion, the dignity of the eucharistic celebration, and Mary, the woman of the Eucharist. Each of these themes is the focus of one of the chapters of this commemorative volume.

The focus of the present chapter of this commemorative volume corresponds to that of the first chapter of the encyclical itself, namely, the Eucharist as a mystery of faith. Here Pope John Paul II provides a profound summary of the main elements of Catholic faith in the Eucharist.

As the sacramental re-presentation of the passion and death of Christ, the Eucharist is Christ's gift of himself and of his saving work (*EdE* 11). The sacrificial meaning of his passion and death is made sacramentally present in the Eucharist (*EdE* 12). Thus the Eucharist is a sacrifice in the strict sense: given for us, but-in the first-place given to the Father (*EdE* 13). Since it is as the living and risen One, that Christ can become the living bread and the bread of life for us, the Eucharist makes his resurrection sacramentally present, along with his passion and death (*EdE* 14). "The sacramental re-presentation of Christ's sacrifice, crowned by the resurrection, in the Mass involves a most special presence," the Holy Father states, quoting Pope Paul VI, "a substantial presence whereby Christ, the God-Man, is wholly and entirely present" (*EdE* 15). By its very nature, this eucharistic sacrifice is directed to the "inward union of the faith with Christ through communion. … The Eucharist is a true banquet" (*EdE* 16). Through this communion, Christ bestows on us the gift of his Holy Spirit (*EdE* 17). In its "eschatological thrust," the Eucharist directs us to our future resurrection (*EdE* 18), unites us to the celestial liturgy of the communion of saints (*EdE* 19) and "plants the seed of living hope" for "a more human world, a world fully in harmony with God's plan" (*EdE* 20).

The Holy Father presents this summary of the fundamentals of Catholic eucharistic faith under the heading, "The Mystery of Faith." In the course of this exposition, he writes at one point: "Truly the Eucharist is a *mysterium fidei*, a mystery which surpasses our understanding and can only be received in faith. … Before this mystery of love, human reason fully experiences its limitations" (EdE 15). In addition to speaking of the mysterium fidei (mystery of faith), Pope John Paul II frequently uses the expressions mysterium paschale (paschal mystery) and mysterium eucharisticum (eucharistic mystery) in *Ecclesia de Eucharistia*. These different uses involve distinctive but interrelated meanings of the richly significant term "mystery." If we ponder them briefly, we will be drawn more deeply into the argument of the encyclical as well as into the mystery of the Eucharist itself.

The Mysteries in the Mystery of Faith

Clearly, something more is at stake in the Holy Father's use of the term "mystery" than in our common usage of the term to refer to what is as yet unexplained or even to what seems unexplainable. We will, of course, expect the "paschal mystery" to be something quite different from a "murder mystery." But we should not exaggerate the difference between the Catholic and common usages of this term. In both cases, our ability to understand and to penetrate a particular reality is being challenged in a significant way. Naturally, we expect the mystery of a whodunit to be revealed in the last pages of the book, but even scientists speak of the continuing mysteries of the universe, of human brain function and, not to mention, of the human heart.

At least in part, what Pope John Paul II, and Catholics generally, mean by the term "mystery" is analogous to these common usages. Thus, when the Holy Father states that "the Eucharist is a mysterium fidei," we are not surprised when he adds that it is "a mystery which surpasses our understanding." But then he goes on to say that it "can only be received in faith." In this way, the Pope points to what is perhaps the most important difference between Catholic and common uses of the term "mystery." When the term is applied to divine things, the mystery is by definition endless. This does not mean that the things of God are permanently or radically unexplainable and unintelligible, but that they are endlessly intelligible and explainable. The mysteries of faith are so deep in their meaning and so awesome in their beauty that they have the power endlessly to attract and to transform the human minds and hearts, lives and communities, where they are pondered, relished and, finally, loved and adored.

It is important to notice that we can speak somewhat interchangeably of the "mystery" and of the "mysteries" of faith. The mystery of faith is nothing less than God himself. Thus, in a crucial sense, the mystery of faith is one because the triune God, who is at the center of this mystery, is one in being and action, comprehending in a single act of knowledge the fullness of his Truth and Wisdom. Through the gift of faith, the believer is rendered able to participate in this divine vision, but always and only according to human ways of knowing. We know God truly, but not in the way that he knows himself. Human understanding of the single mystery of divine truth is thus necessarily plural in structure. It is in this sense that we can speak both of the "mystery of faith"—referring to the single reality of the triune God who is one in being and action, and known by us through the gift of faith—and of the "mysteries of faith"—referring to our way of grasping the diverse elements of the single mystery of God's plan as we experience them in the life of the Church. All the mysteries of faith are facets of the single mystery of faith, which is nothing less than the triune God himself.

THE MYSTERY OF FAITH AS A MYSTERY OF LOVE

These observations help us to follow the argument of the first chapter of the encyclical *Ecclesia de Eucharistia*. Here, as we have noted, Pope John Paul II is especially concerned to exhibit something of the profound interrelationship of the mystery of faith, the paschal mystery and the eucharistic mystery. In the simplest terms, we can say that the eucharistic mystery is the re-presentation of the paschal mystery and that, surpassing human understanding as they do, both mysteries are part of the single mystery of faith and thus can only be received in faith. The divine gift of faith, bestowed on us in baptism and nurtured through the sacramental life of the Church, makes it possible for us to enter into this mystery of faith.

Fundamental to this mystery of faith, as Pope John Paul II has frequently reminded us, is the divine desire to share the communion of trinitarian life with human beings. No one has ever desired anything more than the triune God desires this. God himself has revealed to us (for how could we otherwise have known about it?) that it is this divine desire—more properly, intention and plan—that lies at the basis of everything: creation, incarnation, redemption, sanctification and glory. To look at everything through the eyes of faith—to adopt, as it were, a "God's eye view"—is to see everything in the light of this divine plan. Looking at things this way—looking at them the way God himself has taught us to do—we understand why we were created, why the Word became flesh, why Christ died and rose from the dead, how the Holy Spirit makes us holy, and why we will see God face to face. We were created so that God could share his life with us. God sent his only begotten Son to save us from the sins that would have made it impossible for us to share in this life. Christ died for this purpose, and, rising from the dead, gave us new life. To become holy is to be transformed—through the power of the Holy Spirit at work in the Church—into the image of the Son so that we may be adopted as sons and daughters of the Father. Glory is the consummation of our participation in the communion of the triune God—nothing less than seeing God face to face. The mystery of faith is, finally, a mystery of love.

THE EUCHARISTIC MYSTERY AS A MYSTERY OF FAITH

Applying this perspective to the Eucharist, we may note that, according to St. John's Gospel, the first people to hear Christ proclaim the Eucharist found that the message surpassed their understanding. Some embraced the mystery in faith, but others were put off by it. When they heard Christ say: "I am the living bread that came down from heaven. Whoever eats of this bread will live forever; and the bread that I will give for the life of the world is my flesh," they asked incredulously, "How can this man give us his flesh to eat?" (*Jn* 6:51-52).

How can this be indeed? Although we want to embrace Christ's affirmation in faith, it is instructive to consider how perfectly natural this question is from the human point of view. It is one that is frequently voiced when human beings hear about something that God is said to have done or to be doing. With regard to the Eucharist, it is asked: How can Jesus be really present under the appearances of bread and wine? How can he give us his flesh to eat and his blood to drink? How can the Eucharist be a sacrificial offering? And so on. The initial question "How can this be?" unfolds into a series of questions about the Eucharist.

But suppose that we look at things with the eyes of faith, in the light of the mystery of faith. Suppose that instead of maintaining a human point of view, we adopt the divine point of view. Suppose that we approach these questions as the great theologians of the Catholic tradition have. Suppose, in short, that we look at the Eucharist in the way God looks at it. When we do this, we may find that our troubling "How can this be?" becomes an awestruck and faith-filled "Why not?" We could say that the mystery of the Eucharist becomes "understandable" in some sense when we see it precisely for what it really is, namely, a mystery of faith.

We have seen that, at the heart of the mystery of faith, is God's desire to share his life with us in the most intimate manner. The Catholic tradition has not hesitated to describe this participation in the divine life as a true friendship with God. Given this truth of our faith, is it not, in a sense, appropriate that God should be moved to send his only-begotten Son into the world and, in the breathtaking divine condescension of the incarnation, to take up a human existence to be known and loved among us as Jesus of Nazareth? Was it not fitting, as the Scriptures say, that the Son of Man should offer his life to his Father on the cross in a reconciling sacrifice of love for our sake?

For St. Thomas Aquinas, who has influenced the Holy Father's thinking about the Eucharist, it is but a short step from the incarnation to the Holy Eucharist. In this connection, St. Thomas wrote: "It is a law of friendship that friends should live together. … Christ has not left us without his bodily presence on our pilgrimage, but he joins us to himself in this sacrament in the reality of his body and blood" (*Summa Theologiae III*, 75, 1). In effect, Aquinas is saying that it makes sense, given what we know about God's plan to bring us into the intimacy of his divine life, to leave us the extraordinary gift of the real and substantial presence of his Son in the Eucharist. In the light of the entire mystery of faith, we can see the Eucharist as the gesture of our divine friend. Pope John Paul II writes: "It is pleasant to spend time with him, to lie close to his breast like the Beloved Disciple (cf. *Jn* 13:25) and to feel the infinite love present in his heart" (*EdE* 25).

But there is more. This is a friendship that expressed itself in the ultimate sacrifice of love in which Christ gave his body and blood up for our sake. When he instituted the Eucharist at the Last Supper, "Jesus did not simply state that what he was giving them to eat and drink was his body and blood; he also expressed its sacrificial meaning and made sacramentally present his sacrifice which would soon be offered on the cross for the salvation of all" (*EdE* 12). By overcoming the effects of sin, the sacrificial passion and death of Christ and his glorious resurrection—the paschal mystery—restored our friendship with God. In this connection, the Holy Father makes a striking point: "This sacrifice is so decisive for the salvation of the human race that Jesus Christ offered it and returned to the Father only after he had left us a means of sharing in it as if we had been present there" (*EdE* 11). Not only does our divine friend want to stay with us; he wants to do so precisely in virtue of the power of the paschal mystery which guarantees what must now, always and everywhere, be a reconciled friendship won at the price of his blood.

No wonder that Pope John Paul II could write: "I want once more to recall this truth and to join you, my dear brothers and sisters, in adoration before this mystery: a great mystery, a mystery of mercy. What more could Jesus have done for us? Truly, in the Eucharist, he shows us a love which goes 'to the end' (cf. *Jn* 13:1), a love which knows no measure" (*EdE* 11). ❧

THE CHURCH HAS RECEIVED THE EUCHARIST
FROM CHRIST HER LORD NOT AS ONE GIFT—HOWEVER PRECIOUS—
AMONG SO MANY OTHERS, BUT AS THE GIFT PAR EXCELLENCE,
FOR IT IS THE GIFT OF HIMSELF, OF HIS PERSON IN HIS SACRED HUMANITY,
AS WELL AS THE GIFT OF HIS SAVING WORK.

Ecclesia de Eucharistia (11)

The Holy Father in a moment of prayer in Lebanon, 1997. Opposite: Leading the *Via Crucis* at the Colosseum in Rome, 2002.

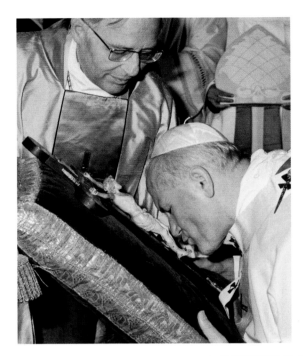

LORD, YOU WILLED THAT ALL THINGS
BE DRAWN TO YOUR SON, MOUNTED ON THE ALTAR OF THE CROSS.
BLESS THOSE WHO DEDICATE THIS ALTAR TO YOUR SERVICE.

Opening Prayer, Rite of Dedication of an Altar

Top left: As Bishop of Rome, the Holy Father venerates a crucifix as he takes possession of his Cathedral, St. John Lateran, 1978. *The altar of the cross.* Top right: The monumental sculpture of Christ Crucified calls to mind simultaneously Christ's sacrifice on the cross and on the altar, Poland, 1983. Bottom: The Patriarchal Basilica of St. Peter, 2001.

THE EUCHARISTIC SACRIFICE MAKES PRESENT
NOT ONLY THE MYSTERY OF THE SAVIOR'S PASSION AND DEATH,
BUT ALSO THE MYSTERY OF THE RESURRECTION WHICH
CROWNED HIS SACRIFICE. IT IS AS THE LIVING AND RISEN ONE
THAT CHRIST CAN BECOME, IN THE EUCHARIST, THE "BREAD OF LIFE"
(*Jn* 6:35, 48), THE "LIVING BREAD" (*Jn* 6:51).

Ecclesia de Eucharistia (14)

Christ is Risen! The pontiff pauses to pray before entering the Patriarchal Basilica of St. Peter, Easter Vigil, 1984.
Next page: The Pope views millions of crosses on a hill in Lithuania, 1993. The Soviet regime completely destroyed
this site three times over fifty years, but the faith of the people prevailed.

TRULY THE EUCHARIST IS A MYSTERIUM FIDEI,
A MYSTERY WHICH SURPASSES OUR UNDERSTANDING AND
CAN ONLY BE RECEIVED IN FAITH ....

Ecclesia de Eucharistia (15)

With a child's heart. A young Nigerian boy receives Communion from the Holy Father in Africa, 1998. In his prayerful hands is his "ticket" for seating at the Papal Mass. Opposite: The Holy Father proclaims Christ "Light of the World" after lighting the Paschal Candle, Easter Vigil, 2002.

DOWN IN ADORATION FALLING THIS GREAT SACRAMENT WE HAIL;
OVER ANCIENT FORMS OF WORSHIP NEWER RITES OF GRACE PREVAIL;
FAITH WILL TELL US CHRIST IS PRESENT, WHEN OUR HUMAN SENSES FAIL.
Liturgy of the Feast of the Body and Blood of Christ

In Adoration. Top left: The Pope prays before the Blessed Sacrament in Lithuania, 1993. Top right: After the distribution of Communion, the Holy Father genuflects as the consecrated hosts are returned to the tabernacle, Oceania, 1986. Bottom: A little girl receives her first Communion from the Pope at the Patriarchal Basilica, 1984.

AND IN THE ROMAN MISSAL THE CELEBRANT PRAYS:
"GRANT THAT WE WHO ARE NOURISHED BY HIS BODY AND BLOOD
MAY BE FILLED WITH HIS HOLY SPIRIT, AND BECOME ONE BODY,
ONE SPIRIT IN CHRIST." THUS BY THE GIFT OF HIS BODY AND BLOOD
CHRIST INCREASES WITHIN US THE GIFT OF HIS SPIRIT,
ALREADY POURED OUT IN BAPTISM AND BESTOWED AS A "SEAL"
IN THE SACRAMENT OF CONFIRMATION.

Ecclesia de Eucharistia (17)

Pentecost Sunday, 1996.

MAY GOD, THE FATHER OF MERCIES,
TO WHOM WE DEDICATE THIS ALTAR ON EARTH,
FORGIVE US OUR SINS AND
ENABLE US TO OFFER AN UNENDING SACRIFICE
OF PRAISE ON HIS ALTAR IN HEAVEN.

Blessing and Sprinkling of Water, Rite of Dedication of an Altar

Greeting the crowd in the Patriarchal Basilica, 1978. *Waiting in joyful hope.* Opposite: The Pope leads the Rosary from his balcony at Castel Gandolfo, his retreat outside Rome, June, 1993. The tapestry depicts the Pentecost.

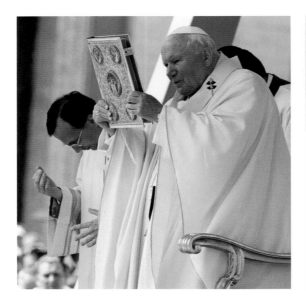

PROSTRATE AT YOUR FEET, O CHRIST,
TODAY WE WANT TO SHARE THE BREAD OF HOPE WITH
OUR BROTHERS AND SISTERS IN DESPAIR;
THE BREAD OF PEACE WITH OUR BROTHERS AND SISTERS TORTURED
BY ETHNIC CLEANSING AND WAR; THE BREAD OF LIFE WITH
OUR BROTHERS AND SISTERS THREATENED EACH DAY BY WEAPONS OF
DESTRUCTION AND DEATH. O CHRIST, WE WANT TO SHARE
THE LIVING BREAD OF YOUR PEACE WITH
THE INNOCENT AND MOST DEFENSELESS VICTIMS.

Pope John Paul II, Feast of the Body and Blood of Christ, 1999

The Eucharist, our refuge and consolation. Top left: The Holy Father at a canonization mass, 2002. Top right: Comforting the sick with Mother Teresa in India, 1986. Bottom left: Offering Eucharistic Benediction for the sick in Portugal, 1982. Bottom right: Distributing Rosaries to children in Barundi, 1990.

MANY PROBLEMS DARKEN THE HORIZON OF OUR TIME.
WE NEED BUT THINK OF THE URGENT NEED TO WORK FOR PEACE,
TO BASE RELATIONSHIPS BETWEEN PEOPLES ON
SOLID PREMISES OF JUSTICE AND SOLIDARITY, AND TO DEFEND
HUMAN LIFE FROM CONCEPTION TO ITS NATURAL END.
AND WHAT SHOULD WE SAY OF THE THOUSAND INCONSISTENCIES
OF A "GLOBALIZED" WORLD WHERE THE WEAKEST,
THE MOST POWERLESS AND THE POOREST APPEAR TO HAVE SO LITTLE HOPE!
IT IS IN THIS WORLD THAT CHRISTIAN HOPE MUST SHINE FORTH!
FOR THIS REASON TOO, THE LORD WISHED TO REMAIN WITH US
IN THE EUCHARIST, MAKING HIS PRESENCE IN MEAL AND SACRIFICE
THE PROMISE OF A HUMANITY RENEWED BY HIS LOVE.
SIGNIFICANTLY, IN THEIR ACCOUNT OF THE LAST SUPPER,
THE SYNOPTICS RECOUNT THE INSTITUTION OF THE EUCHARIST,
WHILE THE GOSPEL OF JOHN RELATES,
AS A WAY OF BRINGING OUT ITS PROFOUND MEANING,
THE ACCOUNT OF THE "WASHING OF THE FEET,"
IN WHICH JESUS APPEARS AS THE TEACHER OF COMMUNION AND
OF SERVICE (CF. *Jn* 13:1–20). THE APOSTLE PAUL, FOR HIS PART,
SAYS THAT IT IS "UNWORTHY" OF A CHRISTIAN COMMUNITY
TO PARTAKE OF THE LORD'S SUPPER AMID DIVISION AND INDIFFERENCE
TOWARD THE POOR (CF. *1 Cor* 11:17–22, 27–34).

Ecclesia de Eucharistia (20)

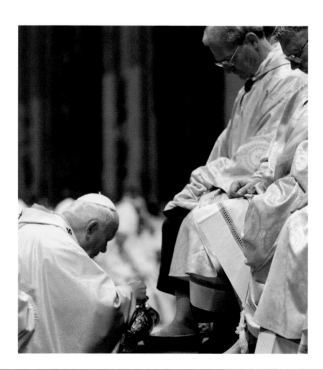

Holy Thursday, 2000.

✠

LET THERE BE AN END TO THE CHAIN OF HATRED AND TERRORISM,
WHICH THREATENS THE ORDERLY DEVELOPMENT OF THE HUMAN FAMILY.
MAY GOD GRANT THAT WE BE FREE FROM THE PERIL
OF A TRAGIC CLASH BETWEEN CULTURES AND RELIGIONS.
MAY FAITH AND LOVE OF GOD MAKE FOLLOWERS OF EVERY RELIGION
COURAGEOUS BUILDERS OF UNDERSTANDING AND FORGIVENESS, PATIENT WEAVERS
OF A FRUITFUL INTER-RELIGIOUS DIALOGUE,
CAPABLE OF INAUGURATING A NEW ERA OF JUSTICE AND PEACE.

Pope John Paul II, Urbi et Orbi Message, Easter 2003

Pacem in terris. Top: The helmet of Fr. Mychal F. Judge, OFM, Conv., who died while administering the Sacraments
to the dying during the September 11, 2001 World Trade Center disaster, is presented to the Pope in November, 2001.
Bottom: The Holy Father tours the results of terrorism in Italy, 1993. Opposite: The Holy Father distributes Holy
Communion at a leper colony in Madagascar, 1989.

WHAT IS GOD'S ALTAR IF NOT THE SOULS OF THOSE WHO LEAD GOOD LIVES?
… RIGHTLY, THEN, THE HEART OF THE JUST IS SAID TO BE THE ALTAR OF GOD.
St. Gregory the Great

At the altar in St. John Lateran, 1999.

THE APOSTLE WROTE, "THE LORD JESUS, ON THE NIGHT WHEN
HE WAS BETRAYED, TOOK BREAD AND WHEN HE HAD GIVEN THANKS,
HE BROKE IT, AND SAID, 'THIS IS MY BODY WHICH IS FOR YOU.
DO THIS IN REMEMBRANCE OF ME.' IN THE SAME WAY ALSO THE CUP,
AFTER SUPPER, SAYING, 'THIS CUP IS THE NEW COVENANT IN MY BLOOD.
DO THIS, AS OFTEN AS YOU DRINK IT, IN REMEMBRANCE OF ME.'
FOR AS OFTEN AS YOU EAT THIS BREAD AND DRINK THE CUP,
YOU PROCLAIM THE LORD'S DEATH UNTIL HE COMES" (*1 Cor* 11:23–26).

WHEN THE CHURCH REPEATS AT EVERY MASS THE WORDS:
"CHRIST HAS DIED, CHRIST IS RISEN, CHRIST WILL COME AGAIN,"
IT IS AS IF SHE TOOK THEM FROM THE LIPS OF THE APOSTLE
TO THE GENTILES TO MAKE THEM HER OWN AND
REPEATS THEM TO THE WHOLE WORLD.

Pope John Paul II, General Audience, June 15, 1995

CHAPTER TWO

THE EUCHARIST BUILDS THE CHURCH

Avery Cardinal Dulles, SJ, STD

The formula, "the Eucharist builds the Church, and the Church makes the Eucharist," which appears in *Ecclesia de Eucharistia* (26) is not new. The formula was used on various occasions by Henri Cardinal de Lubac, whose work presumably influenced the present encyclical.[1] The same idea is implicitly contained in the teaching of Vatican II, *Sacrosanctum Concilium* stating that the Liturgy is both "the summit to which the activity of the Church tends and the font from which all her power flows" (10). In the same article we read that among all liturgical actions, the Eucharist is the principal source of grace and sanctification. The ecclesial fruitfulness of the Eucharist can be better understood if we ponder the inmost nature of the Church herself, variously described as the Body of Christ, the People of God of the New Covenant, the sacrament of unity, and the communion of believers in Christ. All of which can be applied to the Eucharist.

THE CHURCH AND THE EUCHARIST AS THE BODY OF CHRIST

The image of the Church as Body of Christ originates with St. Paul, who declares that all the members of the body, though many, are one body in Christ (*1 Cor* 12:12). He clearly understands that the unity of the ecclesial body has its source in the eucharistic body of Christ. "The bread which we break," he asks, "is it not the body of Christ? Because there is one bread, we who are many are one body, for we all partake of the one bread" (*1 Cor* 10:16–17). The Holy Father, after quoting this text, develops the analogy by quoting St. John Chrysostom on the manner in which the many grains of wheat in the one loaf symbolize the unity of the Church, made up as it is of many persons all incorporated into Christ (cf. *Ecclesia de Eucharistia* 23). For the Church to realize herself as a single sacramental or mystical body, made up of many members animated by the same Spirit, she must nourish herself at the Eucharist. Several years before the present encyclical, Joseph Cardinal Ratzinger expressed the same point. He wrote: "This formula 'The Church is the Body of Christ' thus states that the Eucharist, in which the Lord gives us his body and makes us one body, forever remains the place where the Church is generated, where the Lord himself never ceases to be found anew, in the Eucharist the Church is most compactly herself—in all places, yet one only, just as he is one only."[2]

AVERY CARDINAL DULLES, SJ, is the first U.S. theologian to be named to the College of Cardinals. Cardinal Dulles assisted in the founding of the Intercultural Forum for Studies in Faith and Culture at the Pope John Paul II Cultural Center and lectured there in 2001. A professor at Fordham University and an associate fellow of the Woodstock Center, he has published widely. His current book is entitled *Newman*.

The Church is, in the second place, a sacrament. Vatican II called her a "visible sacrament of saving unity" (*Lumen Gentium* 9). The same may be said of the Eucharist, the supreme sacrament. According to St. Thomas Aquinas and others, the Eucharist is the efficacious sign of the unity of the Church.[3] The presence of Christ, without detriment to its real and substantial nature, may be called mystical or sacramental since it is realized under the forms of bread and wine. The signs, as already mentioned, signify unity, since the bread is one loaf made up of many grains and the wine is one cup from many grapes. "In the sacrament of the eucharistic bread, the unity of the faithful . . . is both expressed and brought about" (*LG* 3; cf. *EdE* 21).

By strengthening the Church in unity, the Eucharist enables the Church to be, like itself, the sacrament of unity. The Church thus becomes the sign of a renewed humanity, used by the Lord as an instrument for the redemption of all (cf. *LG* 9). The Eucharist, standing at the very center of the visible Church, is the vital source of her unitive dynamism. Thirdly, the Church is the new Israel—the people of God of the New Covenant. Through this covenant we are constituted as "a chosen race, a royal priesthood, a holy nation, God's own people" (*1 Pt* 2:9–10). The first Israel was established by the Sinai Covenant, when Moses sprinkled the altar and the people with the blood of goats and bulls (*Ex* 24:8; cf. *Heb* 9:13; also *EdE* 21). Jesus Christ formed the new and definitive Israel by instituting the Eucharist as the New Covenant in his blood, which was to be shed on Calvary (cf. *Mt* 26:28; *1 Cor* 11:25). Just as the Last Supper looked forward to the Crucifixion, the Mass looks back to it and is a renewal of the covenant by which the Church stands. The Church as a covenant people regenerates herself by returning to her own roots.

CHURCH AS COMMUNITY AND EUCHARIST AS COMMUNION

Finally, the Church is a communion; that is to say, a community of believers in Christ, enlivened by his Holy Spirit. According to Vatican II, Christ instituted the Church to bring her members into a communion of life, charity and truth (cf. *LG* 9). Eucharistic Communion brings the members of the Church into such a communion with Christ their Lord. Just as the Eucharist would be incomplete if the sacrificial banquet did not lead to Holy Communion, so too the Church would be incomplete if she did not achieve among her members a communion of grace and love.

The communion among the Church's members within history will always be incomplete and fragile, constantly in need of renewal by sacramental Communion. By means of Holy Communion, the Eucharist prepares the Church to enter into the fullness of communion in the life to come. Pope John Paul II explains this in one of his catechetical lectures: "Especially in the Eucharist and through the Eucharist, the Church contains in herself the seed of a truly universal and eternal communion, the definitive union in Christ of everything in heaven and on earth, as St. Paul has told us (cf. *Eph* 1:10)."[4] The analogy between the Eucharist and the Church could be further explored if we were to reflect on the attributes of the Church. The Holy Father reminds us in Chapter Three of his encyclical that the Creed confesses the Church to be one, holy, catholic and apostolic. He goes on to show how these four attributes are applicable to the Eucharist. One and catholic, the Eucharist is celebrated in all times and places without detriment to its unity. As the real and substantial presence of Christ, the Eucharist is uniquely holy. It is apostolic, especially because the priest-celebrant must be ordained in the apostolic succession.

This essay, focused as it is on Chapter Two of *Ecclesia de Eucharistia*, will leave the four attributes of the Church and the Eucharist to be more fully explored by others.

Editor's note: Cardinal Dulles' article originally appeared in *L' Osservatore Romano*, N.31 – July 30, 2003, and is reprinted here with the kind permission of the paper's editors.

1 Henri de Lubac, *The Splendor of the Church* (San Francisco: Ignatius Press, 1986), 134. This is a translation of the *Meditation sur l' Eglise*, 1953. De Lubac explores the same theme at greater length in his *Corpus Mysticum: L' Eucharistie et l' Eglise au Moyen-Age* (1944).

2 Joseph Cardinal Ratzinger, *Called to Communion* (San Francisco: Ignatius Press, 1996), 37.

3 Thomas Aquinas, *Summa Theologiae*, *III*, qu. 73, art. 2 *sed contra*; cf. art. 3c.

4 General Audience of January 15, 1992, in John Paul II, *The Church: Mystery, Sacrament, Community* (Boston: Pauline Books and Media, 1998), 124.

BY ANALOGY WITH THE COVENANT OF
MOUNT SINAI, SEALED BY SACRIFICE AND
THE SPRINKLING OF BLOOD,
THE ACTIONS AND WORDS OF JESUS
AT THE LAST SUPPER LAID THE FOUNDATIONS
OF THE NEW MESSIANIC COMMUNITY,
THE PEOPLE OF THE NEW COVENANT.

Ecclesia de Eucharistia (21)

HE COMMANDED THE SKIES ABOVE
AND THE DOORS OF HEAVEN HE OPENED;
HE RAINED MANNA UPON THEM FOR FOOD
AND GAVE THEM HEAVENLY BREAD.
MAN ATE THE BREAD OF ANGELS,
FOOD HE SENT THEM IN ABUNDANCE ...

Ps 78

Desert Father. The Holy Father exits the Church of the Transfiguration within the ancient Monastery of St. Catherine on Mt. Sinai, 2000. Next page: Pope John Paul II surveys the "Promised Land" from Mount Nebo, 2000.

THE GIFT OF CHRIST AND HIS SPIRIT
WHICH WE RECEIVE IN EUCHARISTIC COMMUNION
SUPERABUNDANTLY FULFILLS THE YEARNING
FOR FRATERNAL UNITY
DEEPLY ROOTED IN THE HUMAN HEART ...

Ecclesia de Eucharistia (24)

The Holy Father blesses the crowd in Canada, 1987. Opposite: The Pope is welcomed by a sea of people in Portugal, 1982.

BLESS + THIS WATER; SANCTIFY IT.
AS IT IS SPRINKLED UPON US AND UPON THIS ALTAR,
MAKE IT A SIGN OF THE SAVING WATERS OF BAPTISM,
BY WHICH WE BECOME ONE IN CHRIST,
THE TEMPLE OF YOUR SPIRIT.

Blessing and Sprinkling of Water, Rite of Dedication of an Altar

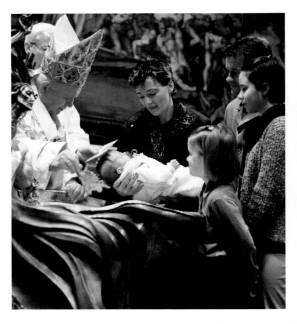

Cleansing waters. Top left: Baptizing a young adult in 2002. Top right: Blessing the crowd in Oceania, 1986.
Bottom left: An infant baptism at the Patriarchal Basilica, 2000. Bottom right: A tender moment in 2000.

THE WORSHIP OF THE EUCHARIST OUTSIDE OF THE MASS IS
OF INESTIMABLE VALUE FOR THE LIFE OF THE CHURCH.
THIS WORSHIP IS STRICTLY LINKED TO THE CELEBRATION OF
THE EUCHARISTIC SACRIFICE. THE PRESENCE OF CHRIST UNDER
THE SACRED SPECIES RESERVED AFTER MASS—
A PRESENCE WHICH LASTS AS LONG AS THE SPECIES OF
BREAD AND OF WINE REMAIN—DERIVES FROM THE CELEBRATION
OF THE SACRIFICE AND IS DIRECTED TOWARD COMMUNION,
BOTH SACRAMENTAL AND SPIRITUAL ...

Ecclesia de Eucharistia (25)

The Holy Father in prayer before an exposition of the Blessed Sacrament in Spain, 1982.

O SALUTARIS HOSTIA
QUAE COELI PANDIS OSTIUM:
BELLA PREMUNT HOSTILIA,
DA ROBUR, FER AUXILIUM.

UNI TRINOQUE DOMINO
SIT SEMPITERNA GLORIA,
QUI VITAM SINE TERMINO
NOBIS DONET IN PATRIA. AMEN.

Top left: In adoration before the Blessed Sacrament in the Patriarchal Basilica of St. Peter, 2002. Top right: In Poland, 1997. Bottom left: In Uganda, 1993. Bottom right: In Slovakia, 1995. Opposite: The Pope raises a monstrance in eucharistic Benediction in Latin America, 1988.

It is pleasant to spend time with him,
to lie close to his breast like the Beloved Disciple
(cf. *Jn* 13:25) and to feel the infinite love present in his heart.
If in our time Christians must be distinguished
above all by the "art of prayer,"
how can we not feel a renewed need to spend time
in spiritual converse, in silent adoration,
in heartfelt love before Christ present
in the Most Holy Sacrament?
How often, dear brothers and sisters,
have I experienced this, and drawn from it strength,
consolation and support!

Ecclesia de Eucharistia (25)

Spiritual reflections while on a mountain hike in Spain, 1989. Opposite: The Pope at prayer, 1991.

> DO YOU WISH TO PRAY? THEN BANISH THE THINGS OF THIS WORLD.
> HAVE HEAVEN FOR YOUR HOMELAND AND LIVE THERE CONSTANTLY—
> NOT IN MERE WORD BUT IN ACTIONS THAT IMITATE ANGELS ...
>
> *Evagrius Ponticus, Chapters on Prayer, 142*

The Holy Father demonstrates any place is suitable for prayer. Top left: Praying the Rosary in a cable car in Poland, 1997. Top right: Praying the Liturgy of the Hours while en route to Mexico, 1979. Bottom: Spending time before the tabernacle outside of Mass in Africa, 1995.

THE BELIEVER, HOWEVER, DOES NOT GIVE UP. HE KNOWS HE CAN
ALWAYS COUNT ON GOD'S HELP. IN THIS REGARD, JESUS' WORDS AT
THE LAST SUPPER SOUND PARTICULARLY ELOQUENT: "PEACE I LEAVE WITH YOU;
MY PEACE I GIVE YOU; NOT AS THE WORLD GIVES DO I GIVE YOU" (JN 14:27).
TODAY WE WANT ONCE AGAIN TO WELCOME AND UNDERSTAND THESE WORDS
IN DEPTH. LET US ENTER INTO THE SPIRIT OF THE UPPER ROOM
TO CONTEMPLATE CHRIST, WHO UNDER THE APPEARANCES OF BREAD AND
WINE GIVES HIS BODY AND BLOOD ...

Pope John Paul II, Feast of the Body and Blood of Christ, 1999

CHAPTER THREE

THE APOSTOLICITY OF THE EUCHARIST AND OF THE CHURCH

Kenneth L. Schmitz, PhD

After they had been with him a while, Jesus sent out the Twelve Apostles to the neighboring towns and villages. With this commission, and the eucharistic gift of himself that seals it, Jesus lays the foundation of what at Pentecost is confirmed as the coming into being of the Church. At the moving heart of Jesus' commission is the mission which—handed down from the Apostles to their successors the bishops—secures the continuity of tradition and the authenticity of witness. For authenticity and mission are inseparable. This act of Jesus, so rich in itself and in its consequences, comprises commission, mission and transmission (*Ecclesia de Eucharistia* 61). Drawing from the *Catechism of the Catholic Church* (857), the letter summarizes the three senses in which the Church is apostolic:

> She was and remains built on the "foundation of the Apostles" (*Eph* 2:20), the witnesses chosen and sent on mission by Christ himself. The Eucharist too has its foundation in the Apostles, not in the sense that it did not originate in Christ himself, but because it was entrusted by Jesus to the Apostles and has been handed down to us by them and by their successors. It is in continuity with the practice of the Apostles, in obedience to the Lord's command, that the Church has celebrated the Eucharist down the centuries. The second sense in which the Church is apostolic, as the *Catechism* points out, is that "with the help of the Spirit dwelling in her, the Church keeps and hands on the teaching, the good deposit, the salutary words she has heard from the Apostles." Here too the Eucharist is apostolic, for it is celebrated in conformity with the faith of the Apostles. At various times in the two-thousand-year history of the People of the New Covenant, the Church's Magisterium has more precisely defined her teaching on the Eucharist, including its proper terminology, precisely in order to safeguard the apostolic faith with regard to this sublime mystery. This faith remains unchanged and it is essential for the Church that it remain unchanged (*EdE* 27). Lastly, the Church is apostolic in the sense that she "continues to be taught, sanctified

KENNETH L. SCHMITZ is Professor of Philosophy Emeritus and Fellow at Trinity College, University of Toronto. Dr. Schmitz assisted in the founding of the Intercultural Forum for Studies in Faith and Culture at the Pope John Paul II Cultural Center and lectured there in 2001. He has written several works on Pope John Paul II, including *At the Center of the Human Drama: The Philosophical Anthropology of Karol Wojtyla/Pope John Paul II.*

and guided by the Apostles until Christ's return, through their successors in pastoral office: the college of Bishops assisted by priests, in union with the Successor of Peter, the Church's supreme Pastor." Succession to the Apostles in the pastoral mission necessarily entails the sacrament of Holy Orders, that is, the uninterrupted sequence, from the very beginning, of valid episcopal ordinations. This succession is essential for the Church to exist in a proper and full sense. The Eucharist also expresses this sense of apostolicity (*EdE* 28).

Apostolicity in these three senses constitutes the faith of the Church in the abiding presence of Christ to her and in her. That faith is expressed in the prayer that joins the Church to its origins and authenticity: "one, holy, catholic and apostolic Church." It is a prayer that is to be uttered in an ecumenical spirit of humility and hope: *ut unum sint.*

Go into the whole world and proclaim the gospel … (*Mk* 16:15)

Given the intrinsic connection between authenticity and apostolicity, it is of great significance that the Twelve were present at the institution of the Eucharist during the Last Supper, for this event binds those who were sent (*apostoloi*), binds them to this most intimate gift of Christ's love. The first and personal meaning of the term "apostle" attaches to the Twelve, though—without jeopardy to this special status, sanctioned by the personal choice of Jesus—it can be and sometimes has been extended to others, whether so-named, nonetheless "sent": such as Matthias who replaced Judas, or those in service with the Apostle Paul: Barnabas, Timothy and, though not so named, there is Philip "sent" to Samaria. The pastoral office of the bishop and the ministerial priesthood is the continuance of that mission, which finds its highest service in the consummation of the Holy Eucharist (*EdE* 1, 3).

Their being sent provides the initial meaning of the term apostle, and custom has tended to reserve it for those first sent. But the term is broader yet, for each member of the Church is an apostle—whether bishop, priest, cleric, religious or layperson. So that apostolicity not only presupposes being a follower of Christ, a learner or disciple, and a witness, but precisely, it is to be one who is sent. To be an ambassador for Christ, one needs to be a disciple and a witness, yet more is needed, and that more is the real presence of the One who sends, himself having been sent by the Father. At the root of apostolicity, then, is the living relation to him who, being sent, sends: it is a special mode of "being-with," and constitutes an intimate co-existence that prefigures the ultimate communion with the Father, Son and Holy Spirit. For it is not that the apostle is with Christ, but rather that Christ is with him and her: in love, in thought, in prayer—and in an especially mysterious way, present in the Eucharist. So that the Eucharist is both an intimate presence with Christ and a being sent to others. At the close of Mass we are called to "go forth and serve the Lord: *Ite, missa est.*"

Now, in this sending and being sent, we come to recognize the pilgrim character of the Church and its members. The encyclical letter *Faith and Reason* (*Fides et Ratio*), speaks of the pilgrim Church which walks with humanity along the pathways of the world (*FeR* 2). In being sent—that is, in being apostolic—both the Church, in its unity, and the faithful, in their diversity, carry with them the gratuity of their origin and the hope of their future. The celebration of Eucharist gathers up time into the dynamic fullness of eternity. For it is the most "present presence" accessible to us—presence intensified, "a most special presence … a presence in the fullest sense" (*EdE* 15). In this presence, the Eucharist gathers up memory and expectation, past and future, origin and destiny into the fullness that transcends the evanescent flow of time.

While the Eucharist is no ordinary meal, it is also no less. The identification of the Eucharist in the liturgy with a sacred meal underscores the care with which Christ "feeds his lambs," and prepares them for their journey through life as his companions and witnesses. The bread is broken and the cup offered to nourish the pilgrims along their ways towards that communion which—even through the impending suffering of the cross—is the hope and the blessing of each and every believer. At Cana, Jesus, at the request of his mother, Mary, turns water into wine to serve the festive spirit; his first miracle, the "first sign" of his Glory (*Jn* 2:3-11). But in the sacrament of the Eucharist, we are sent forth by the One who pours out his life-blood for the world, and provides us—not always with the material commodities we might think we need for the journey—but generously with that spiritual food that is divine life itself.

Our Gospel did not come to you in word alone … (*1 Th* 1:5)

In "hearing" the One who is sent, the recipient not only hears a doctrine preached, however salutary, but receives the real presence of Christ in the Spirit of the New Covenant. This communion is more than the reception of doctrine from an appointed teacher, for the recipient is taken up into the very being of the One who has been sent by the Father: "not I but Christ in me," says St. Paul (cf. *Gal* 2:20).

In his many travels and in his Petrine office, the Holy Father has emulated that "other" Apostle, Paul, whose name he bears—the great missionary *ad gentes*. In bringing Peter to many, as he mirrors and extends the travels of Paul, he reaffirms the communion of their shared apostolates. In giving thanks for the twenty-fifth anniversary of John Paul's elevation to the papal office, we celebrate his succession to Peter, the rock on which the Church is built, and in a personal way we also celebrate the unprecedented manner in which he has been, and continues to be, ambassador to the world. His travels continue to realize apostolicity in an unmatched way, utilizing the global dynamics of the modern world and fusing them with the abiding affirmation of Christ's promise to be with us in every place unto the end of time. Whereas each Christian is called to be an apostle, Pope John Paul II, in the primacy of his papal office, gives fullest expression to the call to apostolicity. He is the apostle among present-day apostles.

In the introduction to the letter on the Eucharist, he recalls his travels in association with the Eucharist:

> When I think of the Eucharist, and look at my life as a priest, as a Bishop and as the Successor of Peter, I naturally recall the many times and places in which I was able to celebrate it. I remember the parish church of Niegowić, where I had my first pastoral assignment, the collegiate church of Saint Florian in Krakow, Wawel Cathedral, Saint Peter's Basilica and so many basilicas and churches in Rome and throughout the world. I have been able to celebrate Holy Mass in chapels built along mountain paths, on lakeshores and seacoasts; I have celebrated it on altars built in stadiums and in city squares. … This varied scenario of celebrations of the Eucharist has given me a powerful experience of its universal and, so to speak, cosmic character. Yes, cosmic! Because even when it is celebrated on the humble altar of a country church, the Eucharist is always in some way celebrated on the altar of the world. It unites heaven and earth. It embraces and permeates all creation. The Son of God became man in order to restore all creation, in one supreme act of praise to the One who made it from nothing. He, the Eternal High priest who by the blood of his cross entered the eternal sanctuary, thus gives back to the Creator and Father all creation redeemed. He does so through the priestly ministry of the Church, to the glory of the Most Holy Trinity. Truly this is the *mysterium fidei* which is accomplished in the Eucharist: the world which came forth from the hands of God the Creator now returns to him redeemed by Christ (*EdE* 8).

The Church is apostolic in the sense that
she "continues to be taught, sanctified and guided by
the Apostles until Christ's return, through their successors
in pastoral office: the college of Bishops
assisted by priests, in union with the Successor of Peter,
the Church's supreme pastor."
Succession to the Apostles in the pastoral mission
necessarily entails the sacrament of Holy Orders,
that is, the uninterrupted sequence,
from the very beginning, of valid episcopal ordinations.
This succession is essential for the Church to exist
in a proper and full sense.

Ecclesia de Eucharistia (28), quoting the Second Vatican Council

In the footsteps of the Fisherman. Pope John Paul II venerates the tomb of St. Peter in the grotto of the Patriarchal Basilica
of St. Peter, 1996. Opposite: The faithful crowd the Patriarchal Basilica in the Holy Year 2000.

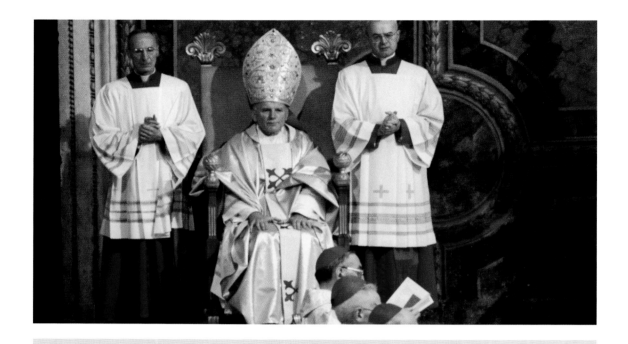

THE EUCHARIST ALSO EXPRESSES THIS SENSE OF APOSTOLICITY.
AS THE SECOND VATICAN COUNCIL TEACHES,
"THE FAITHFUL JOIN IN THE OFFERING OF THE EUCHARIST
BY VIRTUE OF THEIR ROYAL PRIESTHOOD …"

Ecclesia de Eucharistia (24)

Top: The Pope following his election in 1978. Below: St. Peter's statue (foreground, right) seems to give his blessing to an episcopal ordination, 1993.

IF THE EUCHARIST IS THE CENTER AND SUMMIT
OF THE CHURCH'S LIFE, IT IS LIKEWISE THE CENTER AND
SUMMIT OF PRIESTLY MINISTRY. FOR THIS REASON,
WITH A HEART FILLED WITH GRATITUDE TO
OUR LORD JESUS CHRIST, I REPEAT THAT THE EUCHARIST
"IS THE PRINCIPAL AND CENTRAL RAISON D'ÊTRE OF
THE SACRAMENT OF PRIESTHOOD,
WHICH EFFECTIVELY CAME INTO BEING AT THE MOMENT
OF THE INSTITUTION OF THE EUCHARIST."

Ecclesia de Eucharistia (31)

The Pope greets the clergy at the beginning of the Chrism Mass, Holy Thursday, 1984.

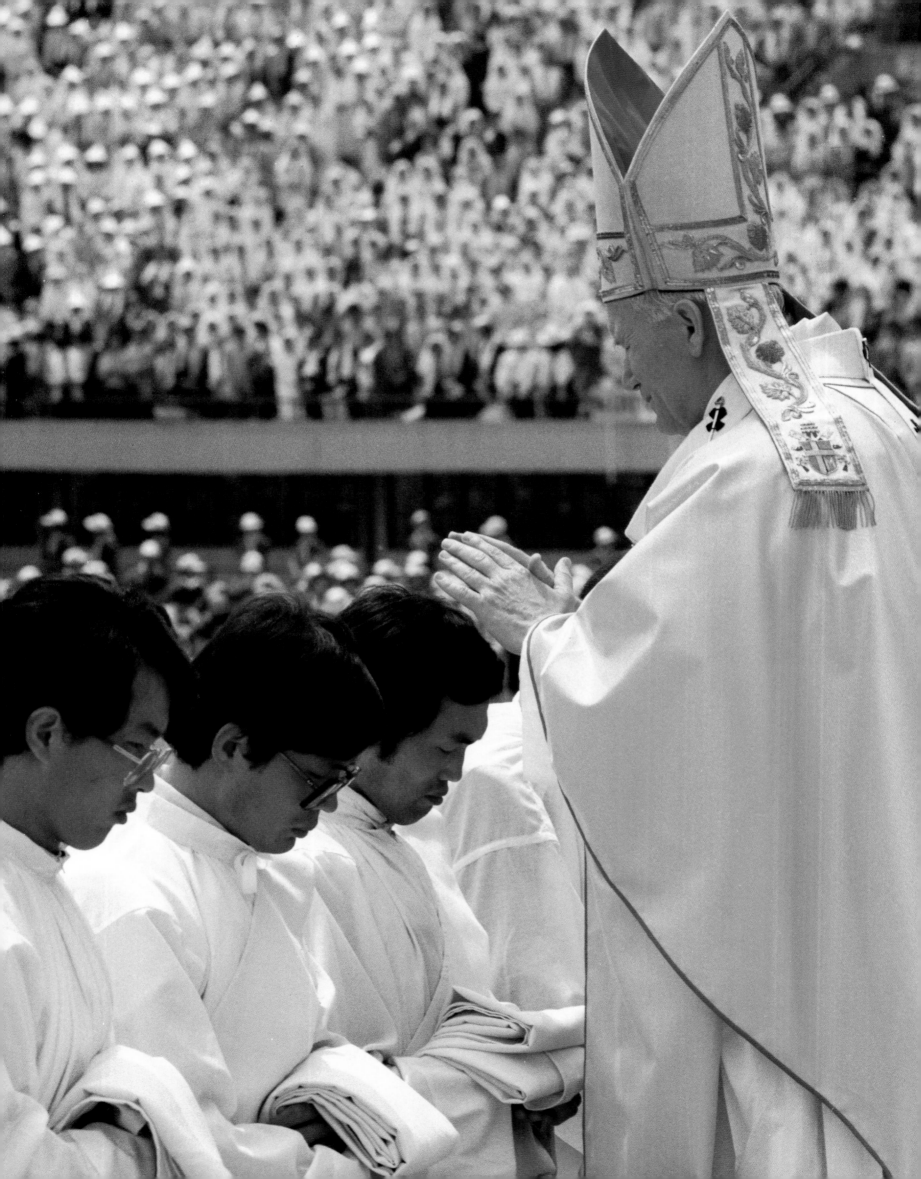

YET IT IS THE ORDAINED PRIEST WHO,
"ACTING IN THE PERSON OF CHRIST, BRINGS ABOUT THE EUCHARISTIC SACRIFICE
AND OFFERS IT TO GOD IN THE NAME OF ALL THE PEOPLE."

Ecclesia de Eucharistia (24)

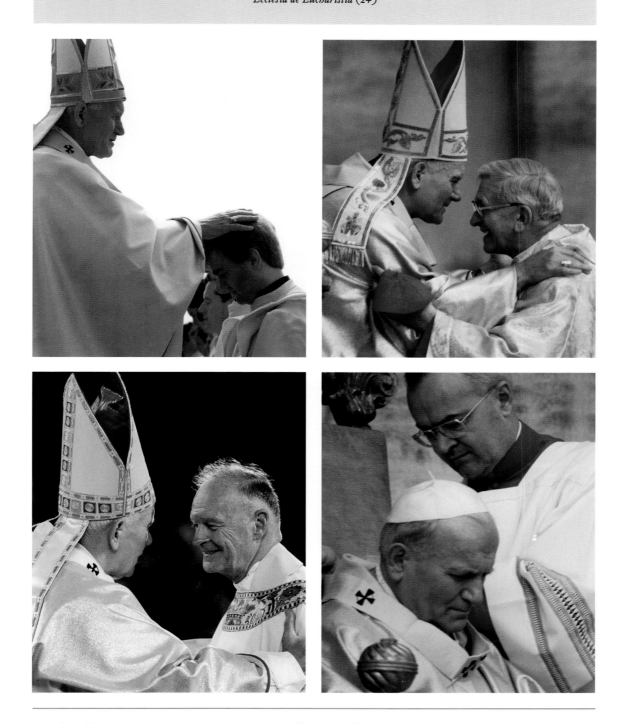

Top left: Ordination in England, 1982. Top right: The pontiff at his installation on October 22, 1978. Bottom left: Theodore Cardinal McCarrick, then Archbishop of Newark, is greeted by the Pope in Newark, 1995. Presently Archbishop of Washington, Cardinal McCarrick was elevated to the College of Cardinals in 2001. Bottom right: The Holy Father receives gemmed pins on his pallium. Opposite: The Sacrament of Holy Orders is administered by the Pope in Korea, 1984.

✦

THE PRIEST, WHO IMITATES THAT WHICH CHRIST DID,
TRULY TAKES THE PLACE OF CHRIST, AND OFFERS THERE IN THE CHURCH
A TRUE AND PERFECT SACRIFICE TO GOD THE FATHER.

St. Cyprian

In unity and love. Top: Mass during the Consistory of May, 2001. Avery Cardinal Dulles is seen far right. Below: Prostrating together in prayer with the Pope at an ordination liturgy in Korea, 1984.

Nourish yourselves, therefore, on the word of God;
converse each day with Christ, truly present in the sacrament
of the Altar. Allow yourselves to be touched by
the infinite love of his Heart and spend more time in
eucharistic adoration in the important moments of your life,
such as difficult personal and pastoral decisions,
at the beginning and end of your day.
I can assure you that I have experienced this,
and drawn from it strength, consolation and support.

Pope John Paul II, Homily, Priestly Ordinations, May 11, 2003

CHAPTER FOUR

THE EUCHARIST AND ECCLESIAL COMMUNION

Richard Schenk, OP, Dr Theol

THE FOCAL POINT: COMMUNION

Among the many dimensions of Ultimate Reality, among the many facets of what is most important in heaven and on earth, some aspects found their thematic expression early in human history. God, Being, the One, the Good, the True, the Eternal have names at least as old as the beginnings of Western thought; indeed, Western thought first crystallized around the attempts to name and discuss these dimensions of Ultimate Reality.

But there were other dimensions of Ultimate Reality that found their way into human attention and human language only slowly and indirectly. Such were Person, Relation, and—the key term of this chapter—Communion. Too important to be overlooked completely, they were seen, so to speak, only from the corner of humankind's eye, perceived in derivative realities, more overlooked than made a center of focus, more horizon than object. "Person" was known in the masks and roles of theatrical performance and in the offices of public service, before the need to express the Christian belief in the Trinity led to a discovery that could apply analogously both to divine and human "persons": the irreducible and irreplaceable (*incommunicabilis*) bearer of a unique dignity and spirituality. Faith in the Trinity helped move "relation" from the status of a trivial "accident" to the core and apex of Reality: What ultimately matters is not so much the autonomy of an isolated One as the towards-one-another or relation of Persons, divine and created. The notions of person and relation, with the spirituality, freedom, dignity, responsibility and solidarity which they imply, would provide one of the important Jewish-Christian sources for Western Civilization, a spur for its development and a measure for its unending task of self-examination and self-critique. They have constituted much of the fulcrum by which Pope John Paul II has attempted to move today's world with the gospel proclamation. The dignity of the person and the quality of the relations that flow from it have been at the heart of his pontificate's message to our times.

Persons can be in a truly interpersonal relation to one another only by sharing something in common; paradoxically, it is a sharing among beings already marked by something too unique to share: the "incommunicable" person of each. The reality of such communion, although a key aspect of Ultimate

RICHARD SCHENK, OP, is the director of the Intercultural Forum for Studies in Faith and Culture at the Pope John Paul II Cultural Center. He is a member of the California province of the Order of Preachers (Dominicans). After doctoral studies in Munich, he taught systematic theology and philosophy in Germany and Switzerland as well as at the Graduate Theological Union in Berkeley, California. From 1991-2000 he was director of the Hannover Institute of Philosophic Research.

Reality, was one of the last to find its way into thematic language and thought. For example, the Greek term for communion/communication/commonality, *koinonia*, played an important but at best secondary role in Aristotle's philosophy of ethics, his study of living the truly good life. Aristotle stressed the ideal of "the great-souled man," the "megalopsychos," marked by a high degree of autonomy and a lack of dependence on others. Despite this emphasis, Aristotle saw that human life could not be said to flourish without friends. Two of the ten books of Aristotle's major work on "Ethics" are therefore devoted to the theme of friendship. And friendship, he notes, is founded upon *koinonia*: commonality and sharing, or communion and communication; without communion, there can be no friendship. If this communion is merely a sharing of common monetary interests, there can be at best business friends. If this communion is merely the shared goal of pleasure, there can be at best an entertaining partnership. But if the "koinonia" is one of common values and shared convictions, this can be the basis of a friendship in the most genuine sense of the term.

St. Thomas Aquinas drew from Aristotle's reflections on friendship to elucidate what the Christian faith understands as charity, including a relationship of humans to God more immediate and more intimate than anything known to the ancient philosophers. A special form of friendship, charity is rooted in the commonality of sacred life. While the Persons of the Triune God share with one another their very being, so even the created persons drawn into the friendship of divine charity share something of the life of God. The grace of faith and charity begins with the grace of a share in divine life. This gift of communion precedes the human responses of faith and charity, which strengthens and personalizes the initial communion in the life of the Trinity. The resulting charity between the believer and God forms the basis for our charity toward other human beings; this good of charity is diffusive of itself. Where others share this faith and charity rooted in divine life, a communion among human beings is built up as the mystical body of Christ, the extension of his life into the wider community. While utilizing directly Aristotle's remarks about friendship and communication, St. Thomas could draw upon and focus the rich biblical and patristic language of communion and sharing, such as the Pauline word that we use to open the eucharistic liturgy: "The grace and peace of our Lord, Jesus Christ, the love of God, and the fellowship (*communication*) of the Holy Spirit be with you all." Communion here is more than the goal of pious or moral effort; it is the source and ultimate goal of the entire world.

EASTERN CHRISTIAN EUCHARISTIC ECCLESIOLOGY

It is telling that the encyclical traces its ideas precisely on communion not to the Latin theologians of the thirteenth-century, otherwise cited several times in the document, nor directly to patristic authors, but to the fourteenth-century Byzantine theologian, Nicolas Cabasilas. The work quoted (34) is not Nicolas' "Interpretation of the Sacred Liturgy," but his study, On Life in Christ. The fourth book of this work, dedicated to the Eucharist, has much to say about the unique, even foundational, character of the Eucharist vis-à-vis the other sacraments, especially about the communion with Christ that we attain in the Eucharist. While the Council of Trent had referred to Nicolas' erudition on the patristic sources for the theology of the sacrificial nature of the Eucharist, the encyclical's reference to his reflections on the unique status of the Eucharist seems to have the subsequent development of Orthodox theology in mind. It is the same ecumenical intent that is reflected in the several citations of Eastern rite liturgies as a source of authentic teaching, a methodological innovation employed already in the Catechism of the Catholic Church, expressing the fruit of ecumenical dialogue during the pontificate of Pope John Paul II between the Roman Catholic Church and the Eastern Orthodox Churches. Even where the sources are older, the frequency and weight of their witness is a mark of this pontificate.

Beginning with the publications of N. Afanasieff (1893-1966) in the 1930s, theologians of the Eastern Orthodox Churches have been developing a "eucharistic ecclesiology," a vision of the Church that takes its foundational idea from a vision of the Eucharist. Central to these eucharistic ecclesiologies is the idea of communion. Included in the idea of eucharistic Communion are the taking of Communion at the Eucharist, the communion with the Triune God, the communion of the local community immediately celebrating the liturgy and, finally, the wider ecclesial communion—the communion with the bishop and the diocese, the communion in teaching, prayer, and charity among local (i.e. diocesan churches), the communion in synods and councils.

The initial intent of N. Afanasieff's programmatic essay of 1934 on "Two Ideas of the Universal Church" set the "eucharistic ecclesiology" against the "universalistic ecclesiology" that he thought expressed the Roman Catholic theology of the Church. The interest in contrasting the two ecclesiologies led Afanasieff to stress initially the local liturgical community at the expense of those wider senses of ecclesial communion that were always implicit in his own thought and certainly of great importance to Orthodox theology as a whole. The subsequent development of this eucharistic ecclesiology, involving Orthodox theologians such as A. Schmemann, J. Meyerdorff, J. Zizioulas, S. Charkianakis and D. Papandreou, as well as Afanasieff himself, has shown a progressively keen sense of the wider implications of communion, moving from an almost exclusive emphasis on the particular community of worship to acknowledge more explicitly that communion of shared belief and of a shared episcopacy needed to frame, to proclaim and to guarantee the belief and worship of a particular congregation. The fruit of this theological resourcement has been a renewed insight into the manifold ways in which eucharistic Communion is embedded in and fosters a broader ecclesial communion.

The success of the Orthodox discussion in wrestling with the temptation to isolate the liturgical community into a self-sufficient monad has made the mature form of this eucharistic ecclesiology accessible to a genuinely Roman Catholic theology of the Church as well. Several previous documents of the Roman Catholic magisterium had made positive references to the fruit of the discussions within the eucharistic ecclesiologies of contemporary Orthodox theologians. The Second Vatican Council (cf. *Lumen gentium*, 4, 8, 13-15, 18, 21, 24-25; *Dei Verbum*, 10; *Gaudium et spes*, 32; *Unitatis redintegratio*, 2-4, 14-15, 17-10, 22), the Second Extraordinary Assembly of the Synod of Bishops in 1985 (cf. *the Relation finalis*, II, C) and the 1992 note of the Congregation for the Doctrine of Faith state, "On some aspects of the Church understood as communion" all reflect the fruit of this ecumenical retrieval of the analogous concept of communion. They gladly take up the insights into the profound and necessary links among Eucharist, a sacramental priesthood, and a strong sense of the episcopacy as fostering the profound reality of the communion that God has chosen to share with humankind. This fourth chapter of the encyclical, "The Eucharist and Ecclesial Communion," must be added to this impressive list of magisterial documents fostering a Roman Catholic reception of eucharistic ecclesiology.

THE CHURCH LIVES FROM THE EUCHARIST

The fourth chapter of the encyclical situates its eucharistic ecclesiology in the context prepared for it by the initial chapters. "The Church lives from the Eucharist" also in the sense that she draws her life from her share (communication) in the mission of Christ (c. 1). This mission is carried out by Christ above all in the sacrifice of the cross (c. 1-2). The extent of the encyclical's emphasis on the work of Christ in the Eucharist can be gauged by the frequency of the term "sacrifice"/"sacrificial," used over seventy times in the encyclical, not counting synonyms such as "offering," "paschal victim" or "blood poured out." The entire encyclical is characterized by its emphasis on the Eucharist as containing the work of Christ "for" humankind (pro vobis et pro multis, for those receiving Communion and for those others whose needs are prayed for by a Church united to Christ's own sacrifice "for" the world in the Eucharist). This includes the encyclical's emphasis on the ways in which the Church draws her life by sharing in this work of Eucharist intercession. Without overlooking the gift of the real presence of Christ in the Eucharist, the encyclical is even more concerned with recalling the ways in which the real presence of Christ involves the Church ever anew in his unique and ultimate sacrifice, the definitive source of all perfected communion. The Eucharist is apostolic in the sense that it, too, is for ("pro") others; the further modes in which the Eucharist is apostolic (c. 3) are given to the Church to support her basic apostolic mission of eucharistic "pro-existence." This communion in Christ's offering (pro vobis et pro multis) means that the

Church is a leaven, a communion, which fosters the growth of that communion—with the Triune God and among all peoples. Neither the vertical nor the horizontal dimension of this communion, neither the invisible nor the visible notes of eucharistic Communion (*Ecclesia de Eucharistia* 35-38), could be lost without losing the Church herself. The communion of life, mission, sacrifice and apostolate that the Church shares with her Lord is meant to increase humankind's communion in God's own life.

The same Christ who is uniquely present in this unique sacrament is also the source of a further, unique grace. In the Eucharist, the really present Lord is both our ultimate good and the Savior of the penultimate goods that reflect him; he is both *res et sacramentum*. Most other sacraments are for the recipients themselves; for example, the prayers of petition added to the rite of baptism do not belong to the essence of that sacrament itself. But, in the Catholic understanding of the Eucharist (admittedly, not one shared by all ecclesial communities), praying for others in the sacrifice of the Mass belongs to the very heart of the Eucharist. Beyond the immediate gift offered to those perceiving and receiving the sacrament, the Lord's sacrifice made present in the Eucharist is meant as an effective blessing for others: *pro vobis et pro multis*. When making the needs and wounds of the world transparent to the passion of Christ, bringing them in the power of the Spirit before the Father, the eucharistic Church is granted a share in the "pro-existence" of Christ's sacrifice on the cross. "In this gift Jesus Christ entrusted to his Church the perennial making present of the paschal mystery" (*EdE* 5). In the penultimate sentence uttered before he was assassinated during Mass, Bishop Oscar Romero gave final witness to this Catholic understanding of Eucharist: "May this body, given over to the sacrificial fire, and may this blood, sacrificed for humankind, so nourish us, that we, too, might hand over our body and blood to suffering and pain, but as Christ did, not for ourselves, but in order to attain justice and peace for our people" (Oscar Romero, *Voice of the Voiceless* [Maryknoll, NY: Orbis, 1985], 193).

The Ecclesial Communities of the Reformation

In the interests of continuing the Church's existence and mission as communion and a sacrament of Communion, the encyclical shows not only the fruits but also the limits of recent ecumenical convergence. The contrast to the understanding of the Eucharist in several ecclesial communities of the Reformation remains stark. One of the most respected theologians of the Reformational communities, Eberhard Juengel, expressed an alternative, genuinely Lutheran view as follows:

> Whenever we come together for the celebration of the Lord's Supper, what's at stake is our very being as being together with God; and nothing else. In the Lord's Supper no demand is heard that would require deeds of us. The law that issues commands falls silent here. Here there is no room for the demanding Imperative. Here rules alone that Indicative of the gospel from which grace flows. This is the Indicative which transforms us from actors to recipients, which takes human beings from whom much, and even too much, is demanded, and makes them again into beings, who are glad that they are able to exist, glad that they are able to be together with Jesus Christ and so also with one another .... [Thus] it remains unfortunate that the Roman Catholic Church following Trent continues to speak widely of the sacrificial action of the priest or of the Church. On the contrary: the self-sacrifice of Christ calls precisely not for our sacrifice, it does not call for us to do anything, but rather it calls for us to receive, although from this receptivity Christian action does result—just as the work week results from the creative passivity of the Sabbath. (Eberhard Juengel, "The Unity of the Church is Already Happening: On the Path towards Eucharistic Community." [Address at the 93rd German Katholikentag, 12 June 1998, in Mainz. Trans. from the German text pub. in *Katholische Nachrichten Agentur* (KNA). Oekumenische Information, 14 July 1998])

As Juengel clarifies here and in his magisterial work of the same year on the Lutheran understanding of justification, this understanding of the Lord's Supper is linked necessarily to an understanding of justification as remaining purely receptive (*mere passiva*) and to the denial of any major difference between the ordained priesthood and the priesthood of all the faithful. All three of these interconnected teachings may be assigned the status accorded the doctrine of justification as an article of faith by which the Church stands or falls. The Eucharist celebrated in each church or ecclesial community is the expression of what these understands themselves—and Christian existence—to be. Communicants confess that understanding in their reception of Communion. So, too, the *Common Declaration on Justification* (*CDJ*) of 1999 was not able to resolve the differences between the Lutheran and Roman Catholic communities on Eucharist and ministry or on the issues of justification most directly associated with them (cf. e.g. *CDJ* 43 and notably the references to the sacrament of reconciliation in the *Eucharistic Encyclical* 36-37, as well as the basic message of the encyclical regarding the Church as called to share here in the work of Christ).

COMMUNIO

The lack of visible unity painfully evident in the present impossibility of intercelebration is itself a powerful call to renewed efforts at increased ecclesial communion (*EdE* 44). Between the personal and the universal fruits of the eucharistic sacrifice, this goal of Church unity is central to the encyclical (cf. *EdE* 23-24); it is also characteristic of the entire pontificate. Aiming at the unity of the many (communio), it is here in the Eucharist that disunity, too, is most acutely felt. One of the primary concerns of the entire encyclical, the implications of ecclesial communion for the concrete possibilities of eucharistic intercommunion, is a special topic of the chapter (*EdE* 43-46). Already St. Augustine has stressed that the Eucharist provided us access not only to Christ's own body (the corpus Christi verum), but to the peace and unity of the Church which is his gift (the corpus Christi mysticum); our love of the one demands our love of the other.

The Catholic understanding of the sacrificial character of the Eucharist, its pro-existence, its transformative powers, and the ministerial implications of its apostolicity as well as its role as the expression and instrument of communion show the limits of a simply convergent or conformistic ecumenism. Intercommunion and intercelebration with those Christian communities that deny these dimensions of the Eucharist (*EdE* 45-46) would in fact mean for the Church a "closing in upon herself," the reduction of her pro-existence for the world. It is of benefit to the Church's wider mission that a conformism be avoided which would conceal or even renounce the sacrificial ministry of the Eucharist.

This need for distinction does not deny that Roman Catholic theologians have much to learn precisely from many of the ecclesial communities of the Reformation; in particular, a new sensibility for the vision of Christ as the principal subject acting in the sacraments could be gained by further ecumenical discussion. Without losing sight of the ways in which the Church is called to active cooperation in the Eucharist, a renewed Catholic theology of the Eucharist (cf. *EdE* 15) could learn from the most genuine theologies of the Reformation to resist the temptation to an anthropological-sociological reduction of the sacraments to the celebration merely of a local human community (cf. *EdE* 12), reaffirming, rather, the activity of Christ in the sacraments as their primary subject.

Above all, the Eucharist, which, in offering Christ's own body, also contributes to the unity of the Church as his mystical body, is an especially blessed place, where for the most fitting unity and the fullest integrity of the Church should be prayed for: "... and grant her the peace and unity of your kingdom where you live forever and ever." As St. Augustine expressed it: "Take and eat the body of Christ, becoming in that body of Christ members of his body. Take and drink the blood of Christ, not casting off but taking in the bonds of your unity. Recognize your dignity, drink your price .... Thus you begin to receive what you begin to be" (*Sermo* 227, *PL* 38, 1099-1101).

THE TWO SACRAMENTS OF THE EUCHARIST AND PENANCE
ARE VERY CLOSELY CONNECTED.
BECAUSE THE EUCHARIST MAKES PRESENT
THE REDEEMING SACRIFICE OF THE CROSS,
PERPETUATING IT SACRAMENTALLY,
IT NATURALLY GIVES RISE TO A CONTINUOUS NEED
FOR CONVERSION, FOR A PERSONAL RESPONSE TO THE APPEAL
MADE BY SAINT PAUL TO THE CHRISTIANS OF CORINTH:
"WE BESEECH YOU ON BEHALF OF CHRIST,
BE RECONCILED TO GOD" (*2 COR* 5:20).
IF A CHRISTIAN'S CONSCIENCE IS BURDENED BY SERIOUS SIN,
THEN THE PATH OF PENANCE THROUGH THE SACRAMENT
OF RECONCILIATION BECOMES NECESSARY
FOR FULL PARTICIPATION IN THE EUCHARISTIC SACRIFICE.

Ecclesia de Eucharistia (37)

Bless me, Father ... the Pope prepares to hear confession at the Patriarchal Basilica of St. Peter, 2000. Opposite: The Holy Father begins Lent as he does each year by receiving ashes at Santa Sabina in Rome, 2002.

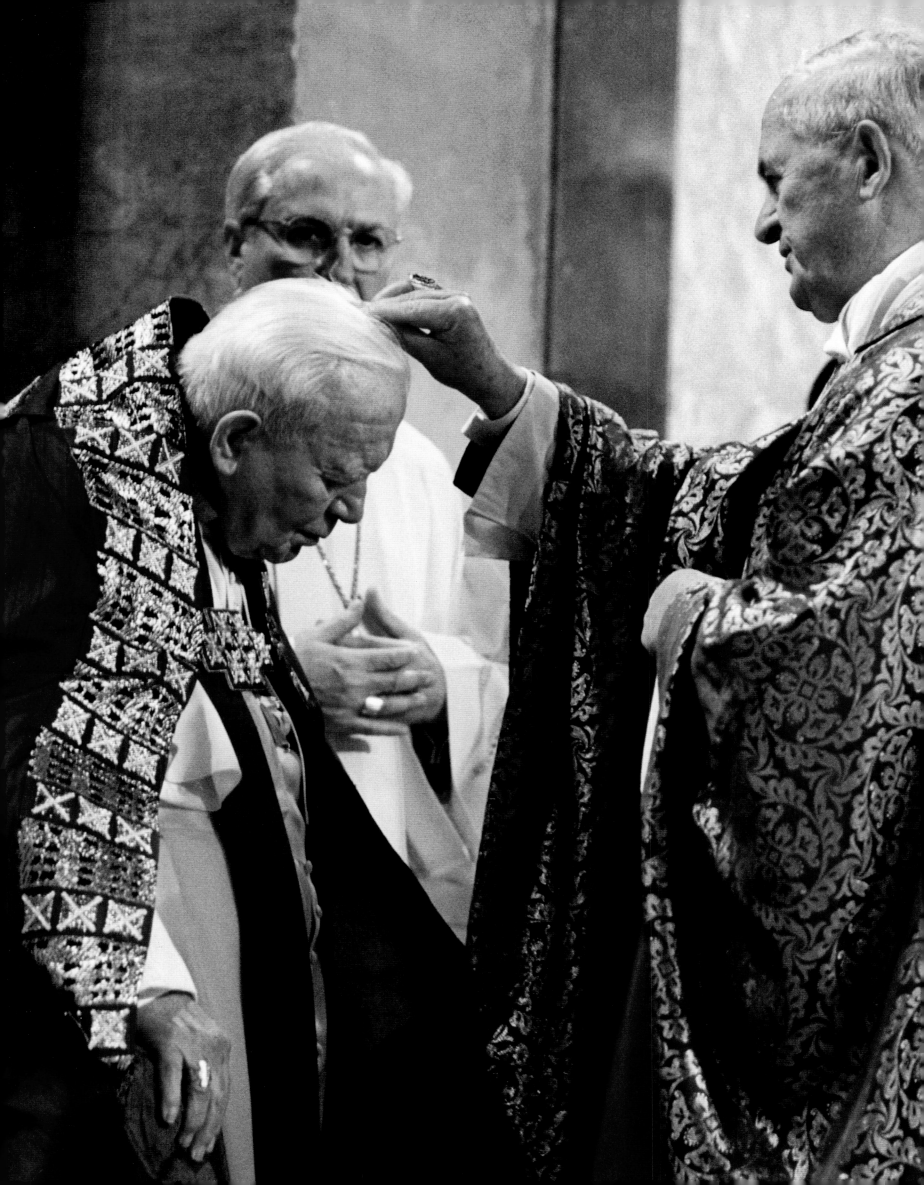

I WILL POUR CLEAN WATER OVER YOU AND WASH AWAY
ALL YOUR DEFILEMENT. A NEW HEART WILL I GIVE YOU, SAYS THE LORD.
Ezek 36:25-26

Prayers for unity. Top: The world's religious leaders gather in Assisi to pray for peace, 1986. St. Francis' Portiuncula can be
seen in the background. Below: Later that day, the Holy Father is joined by the Ecumenical Patriarch of Constantinople,
Demetrios I (left), and the Archbishop of Canterbury, Robert Runcie.

> Make [this altar] a source of unity and friendship,
> where your people may gather as one to share your spirit of mutual love.
>
> *Prayer of Dedication, Rite of Dedication of an Altar*

An instrument of God's peace. The world's leaders and the Pope. Top left: With Fidel Castro in Cuba, 1998. Top right: Michail Gorbacev, 2000. Bottom left: Poland's President Aleksander Kwasniewski, 2002. Bottom right: Nelson Mandela, 1998. Next page: Argentina, 1982.

Believers draw from the presence of
the Risen Lord the courage to be agents of solidarity and renewal,
responsible for changing the structures of sin in which individuals,
communities and sometimes entire peoples are trapped.

Pope John Paul II, International Eucharistic Congress, June 2000

The Pope at Gadansk, Poland, 1987.

JEWS AND CHRISTIANS SHARE AN IMMENSE SPIRITUAL PATRIMONY,
FLOWING FROM GOD'S SELF-REVELATION. OUR RELIGIOUS TEACHINGS AND
OUR SPIRITUAL EXPERIENCE DEMAND THAT WE OVERCOME EVIL WITH GOOD.
WE REMEMBER, BUT NOT WITH ANY DESIRE FOR VENGEANCE OR
AS AN INCENTIVE TO HATRED. FOR US, TO REMEMBER IS TO PRAY
FOR PEACE AND JUSTICE, AND TO COMMIT OURSELVES TO THEIR CAUSE.
ONLY A WORLD AT PEACE, WITH JUSTICE FOR ALL,
CAN AVOID REPEATING THE MISTAKES AND TERRIBLE CRIMES OF THE PAST.

Pope John Paul II, Yad Vashem Holocaust Memorial, Jerusalem, March 23, 2000

Our elder brothers in faith. Top left: The Pope at Jerusalem's Western Wall, 2000. Top right: Receiving Holocaust survivors in Poland, 1979. Bottom: The Holy Father distributes Holy Communion at an outdoor Mass, 1997.

OUR LONGING FOR THE GOAL OF UNITY
PROMPTS US TO TURN TO THE EUCHARIST,
WHICH IS THE SUPREME SACRAMENT
OF THE UNITY OF THE PEOPLE OF GOD,
IN AS MUCH AS IT IS THE APT EXPRESSION
AND THE UNSURPASSABLE SOURCE
OF THAT UNITY.

Ecclesia de Eucharistia (43)

East meets West. The Holy Father leaves the Ecumenical Patriarch's palace in Istanbul, 1979. Opposite: Romanian Patriarch Teocist joins the Pope in Rome, 2002.

MAKE [THIS ALTAR] A PLACE OF COMMUNION AND PEACE,
SO THAT THOSE WHO SHARE THE BODY AND BLOOD OF YOUR SON
MAY BE FILLED WITH HIS SPIRIT AND GROW IN YOUR LOVE.

Prayer of Dedication, Rite of Dedication of an Altar

Brothers in Christ. Top: Karekin II, Catholicos of All Armenians, joins the Holy Father at the Patriarchal Basilica, 2000.
Below: Greek Orthodox Metropolitan Christodoulos with the Pope beneath an icon of St. Paul in Athens, 2001.

I WOULD LIKE NONETHELESS TO REAFFIRM WHAT I SAID IN MY
ENCYCLICAL LETTER *Ut Unum Sint* AFTER HAVING ACKNOWLEDGED
THE IMPOSSIBILITY OF EUCHARISTIC SHARING: "AND YET WE DO HAVE A BURNING DESIRE
TO JOIN IN CELEBRATING THE ONE EUCHARIST OF THE LORD, AND THIS DESIRE
ITSELF IS ALREADY A COMMON PRAYER OF PRAISE, A SINGLE SUPPLICATION.
TOGETHER WE SPEAK TO THE FATHER AND INCREASINGLY WE DO SO WITH ONE HEART."

Ecclesia de Eucharistia, (44)

Toward Communion. Top left: The Holy Father with the Russian Orthodox Patriarch, 1980. Top right: Signing an accord in Romania with Romanian Orthodox Patriarch Teocist, 1999. Bottom: Welcoming Greek Orthodox Patriarch Bartholomew I at the Vatican, 1995. Next page: The Pope in a eucharistic procession through the streets of Rome, 2002.

I WOULD LIKE TO RECALL THE DAY OF PRAYER FOR
WORLD PEACE HELD IN ASSISI ONE YEAR AGO, ON 24 JANUARY.
THAT INTER-RELIGIOUS EVENT SENT A POWERFUL MESSAGE TO THE WORLD:
EVERY AUTHENTICALLY RELIGIOUS PERSON IS OBLIGED TO ASK GOD
FOR THE GIFT OF PEACE, WITH RENEWED DETERMINATION
TO PROMOTE AND BUILD PEACE TOGETHER WITH OTHER BELIEVERS.
THE THEME OF PEACE REMAINS AS URGENT AS EVER.
IT MAKES PARTICULAR DEMANDS ON THE FOLLOWERS OF CHRIST,
THE PRINCE OF PEACE, AND IT REPRESENTS A CHALLENGE AND
A COMMITMENT FOR THE ECUMENICAL MOVEMENT.

Pope John Paul II, Concluding Vespers for the Week of Prayer for Christian Unity, January 25, 2003

The Dignity of the Eucharistic Celebration

Francis Cardinal George, OMI, STD, PhD

Art Gives Form to the Truth of Divine Reality

"The world will be saved by beauty," said the Russian writer Dostoevsky. That profound truth is at the heart of Catholic, as well as Orthodox, theological and liturgical understanding. St. Paul could speak to the Christians of Corinth of "the knowledge of God's glory shining in the face of Christ" (*2 Cor* 4:6). The preface of the Mass of Christmas sings of the enrapturing light of the Trinitarian life streaming forth from the glorious form of Jesus Christ.

The unfolding bloom of a rose can speak of beauty that seems inexpressible, unattainable. Yet the rose represents a mystery infinitely inferior to the mystery of Christ. The Christ event that goes so utterly beyond all human imagination reaches an apogee in the Eucharist. "That God's love would invent this unique way of communicating itself through the sign of bread, the food of the poor! Of all the gifts of Christianity displayed in front of me, this was the most beautiful," exclaimed the journalist Andre Froissard when he was a new convert to Catholicism.

In this encyclical, the Holy Father challenges us to recapture "amazement" before "the unsurpassable gift of the Eucharist" (*Ecclesia de Eucharistia* 5). As Catholic people over many ages have savored the intensity of the eucharistic presence and the sacrificial action that is the heart of the Mass, the Church has composed the canons, collects and other prayers which have acquired a patina of great beauty that expresses powerfully the wonder of the mystery. At the same time, the perennially new and immeasurable depth of the divine event sacramentally re-presented has inspired works of matchless earthly beauty: painting, architecture and music in the great tradition of the Church. Through these, the believer encounters the glory of the Father that shines in the face of Christ. Their beauty leads beyond the aesthetic to the holy and divinely glorious.

In the Holy Father's words, "the Church has feared no 'extravagance,' devoting the best of her resources to expressing her wonder and adoration" before the eucharistic sacrifice that is "the source and summit of the Christian Life" (*Lumen Gentium* 11). It is the "waste" of what is precious and valuable, taken from mundane use, to speak of what is valuable beyond earthly measure—the gold of the sacred vessels, the precious marble of the altar, the pure linen of the cloths, the candles which consume

Francis Cardinal George is the Archbishop of Chicago and assisted in the founding of the Intercultural Forum for Studies in Faith and Culture at the Pope John Paul II Cultural Center. His Eminence holds a PhD in American philosophy and among his numerous articles and books is *Inculturation and Ecclesial Communion*.

themselves in symbol of divine self-giving and inviting our self-offering. These are, says the Holy Father, "the outward forms meant to evoke and emphasize the grandeur of the event being celebrated" (*EdE* 49). To give perceptible sense to the mystery, the sacramental reality of the Eucharist is embodied in ritual which "weaves speech, gesture, rhythm and structured ceremonial into a form of worship expressive of the human person's being in the world. It unites our physical, mental and emotional being in a single response to the unseen …" (Aidan Nichols, *Epiphany*, 278).

The liturgy conditions the way we perceive the Eucharist by maintaining an attitude of reverence, as the Church seeks "to celebrate the Eucharist in a setting worthy of so great a mystery" (*EdE* 48). The various rites of the liturgy foster a sense of the eucharistic mystery that holds together inward devotion and the forms that evoke the event being celebrated. The Eucharist has the shape of a banquet, a meal, but one that is quite out of the ordinary; it is a sacred and sacrificial banquet. The food we receive in the Eucharist is the bread of wayfarers, but it is always the bread of angels, never to be trivialized by reducing it to an ordinary meal. The heritage of music, architecture, painting and sculpture that has come to surround it fulfills a similar function. It is not simply art but, with a clear perception of the eucharistic mystery, it is art mediating faith, a medium of mystery.

The liturgy of the Eucharist is not to be reduced to simple catechesis or to a pedagogical instrument. The liturgy makes present Christ, the giver of salvation and the source of holiness. It is not legitimate to oversimplify it or to rationalize it in the spirit of the eighteenth-century Enlightenment. There is a polyphonic quality to the Catholic eucharistic rites; they have levels of meaning, as they are handed down in the Church. The liturgy has to be complex because it embodies what is of God. In recent reforms, often too little attention was paid to the sacramental complexity of the liturgy. Nor has the situation always been helped by those seeking to restore forms of worship from a "golden age." At times the claimed return to the sources was so narrow as to become a new kind of fundamentalism. Recent historical re-thinking shows that some of the reshaping of the liturgy done in the name of Vatican II was superficial and wanting in adequate scholarly justification.

The time has come, the Holy Father is telling us both in the present encyclical and other official documents, to re-think the practical meaning of the famous "noble simplicity" called for by Vatican II and to understand that it has to be much more than modernistic austerity. This encyclical is challenging us to rediscover at a deep level the symbols with which the Church has loved to surround the Holy Sacrifice and the Blessed Sacrament; some of them have been set aside too lightly.

The encyclical, together with the newly revised *General Introduction to the Roman Missal*, offers an opportunity to put things into larger perspective. It is precisely in a spirit of gratitude and amazement at the wonder of the Eucharist that the Holy Father is inviting the Church—at this point of transition in her history and in the history of the world—to be open to the new without letting go of her inherited culture of worship and Christian experience. It is the remarkable gift of the encyclical that it proposes for our encouragement the loving, happy, secure spirit of the Pope's own eucharistic faith that can set us free from ideologies whose time has passed and which have no future in theology, in liturgy or in art. The Pope challenges us to find liberty of spirit in the "forms" chosen by the Church's great liturgical tradition (*EdE* 52) and her magisterium. He invites us to stop revolting against "formalism" and not to inflict on the faithful "a misguided sense of creativity and adaptation" and the "unauthorized innovations which are often completely inappropriate" (*EdE* 52).

It is a question of being more open to what is given: individual creativity finally is not an authentic category for the communal celebration of the eucharistic liturgy. The Eucharist is itself revelation, divine gift, not spontaneity or improvisation. The symbols have to be accepted for what Christ made them to be, which always goes beyond what can be explicitly stated. Development of the liturgical rites has to go in the direction of greater density, of the more complex, whose ceremonies, language and chanted formulae mark off worship from prosaic things. The task is "to repossess the inheritance of the past in a distinctively modern way and to reorganize it on a basis that seems intellectually satisfying and pastorally helpful" (Aidan Nicholas, *The Shape of*

Catholic Theology, 198). The Church lives in the present for the future in light of the Tradition which unites her to Christ. The Church from the Eucharist lives from the "holy banquet in which Christ is received, the memory of his passion is renewed, the soul is filled with grace and a pledge of future glory is given to us" (St. Thomas Aquinas, *O sacrum convivium*).

ART REVEALS THE INNER BEAUTY

In speaking of the dignity of the eucharistic celebration, the Holy Father refers to his 1999 *Letter to Artists*. There he described the vocation of the artist "to express the inner beauty of things." The religious artist responds to the interplay of God's beauty made present and visible in Jesus Christ, because "beauty," says the Holy Father, "is the key to the mystery."

That point is also made by the *Catechism of the Catholic Church* as it explains that truth, which is beautiful in itself, finds expression in the language of creation. Art then becomes a language of beauty to give form to the truth of reality and of the revealed mystery of God. "Sacred art is true and beautiful when its form corresponds to its particular vocation: evoking and glorifying, in faith and adoration, the transcendent mystery of God—the surpassing invisible beauty of truth and love visible in Christ, who 'reflects the glory of God and becomes the very stamp of his nature,' in whom 'the whole fullness of deity dwells bodily'" (*Catechism of the Catholic Church* 2502).

I saw an example of artistic beauty at the service of eucharistic mystery when, a couple of years ago, during a visit to Poland, I walked into the Blessed Sacrament chapel in the Cathedral of Wroclaw. There one sees in sculpture, painting and architecture what we believe about the presence of Christ through this sacrament. The Blessed Sacrament is reserved in a cask modeled after the description of the Ark of the Covenant which contained the presence of God among his chosen people on the journey to the Promised Land and was finally brought by King David into Jerusalem (*2 Sam* 6). On each side of the tabernacle, fashioned as an ark, are statues of Moses and Aaron. Moses governed the people and Aaron offered sacrifice for them as their priest. The intent of the arrangement is clear. God has dwelled with his people, was present to them in the first Covenant and he has found a unique way to be present to them, through Christ, shepherd and priest, in the New Covenant.

On the side walls of that chapel in the Wroclaw Cathedral, two paintings face each other. One depicts Jesus at the Last Supper; the other shows Melchizedek, King of Salem, offering bread and wine before Abraham (*Gen* 14:18-20). Again, the meaning is clear; the priesthood instituted at the Last Supper reaches back behind Aaron to Abraham and, further back, to the covenant with Noah. It is not a continuation of the Levitical priesthood but is more universal in its antecedents and origin.

Finally, the chapel contains four doors. Above each is a sculpture of one of the four last things: death, judgement, heaven and hell. Through the doors of death and judgement we pass, if we have not deliberately destroyed our relationship to Christ by mortal sin, to the eternal banquet which begins here in the eucharistic banquet, the sacrifice of the Mass. The chapel is a remarkable exposition of the mystery of the Eucharist.

Sacred art today seems sometimes affected by the general separation of the world of art from the world of faith. The Holy Father, in his 1999 *Letter to Artists*, saw signs of hope: "Even in situations where cultures and the Church are far apart, art remains a kind of bridge to religious experience .... Even when they explore the darkest depths of the soul or the most unsettling aspects of evil, artists give voice in a way to the universal desire for redemption" (*Letter to Artists* 10).

The separation between art and faith has deep roots, going back to the separation of faith from many areas of life in this process of secularization in the West. Along with diminished belief in God has come a loss of a sense of the good's relation to the beautiful. This loss conditions artists' understanding of themselves and of all human beings. At a recent exhibition in a major London gallery, a chief exhibit was an unmade bed; in the recent Venice Biennale an exhibition of corpses was a high point. Art ends in a trivialization which becomes sinister. The inner beauty of the human person as well as the beauty of the mysteries of faith often lack means of artistic expression today.

Hans Urs von Balthasar points out that, without beauty, both goodness and truth are destabilized. In a world without beauty, truth loses the power to convince and then good loses the power to attract (Robert Sokolowski, *Presence and Absence*, 207). Art is then not capable of producing a Blessed Sacrament chapel to match that of Wroclaw Cathedral. For the sake of art itself, for the sake of the Church, the Holy Father calls for a new alliance between the Church and artists "in order to communicate the message entrusted to the Church by Christ" (*LtA* 12) and to achieve "a renewed 'epiphany' of beauty in our time" (*LtA* 10). In the search for new artistic forms, the Church will have to lead by pointing to her tradition and to the beauty, truth and goodness it embodies. In the Letter to Artists, the Holy Father evoked the example of the masterpieces of various ages when faith helped create the climate in which artists were able to "render visible the perception of the mystery which makes of the Church a universally hospitable community, mother and traveling companion to all men and women in their search for God" (*LtA* 9).

In *Ecclesia de Eucharistia*, the Holy Father asks that, in the service of the Church, artists display not only technical skill but "show themselves open to the inspiration of the Holy Spirit. Sacred art must be outstanding for its ability to express adequately the mystery grasped in the fullness of the Church's faith and in accordance with the guidelines appropriately laid down by competent authority" (*EdE* 50). In various cultures, different forms and styles can be adapted to express something of the wonder and holiness of the Eucharist, provided that this be done "with a constant awareness of the ineffable mystery against which every generation is called to measure itself" (*EdE* 51).

God's Dwelling with the Human Race (*Rev* 21:3)

The Eucharist has inspired great architecture, fruit of genuine artistic inspiration rooted in an understanding of the mystery of faith. That understanding of mystery remains both a criterion for judging the quality of church architecture and a continuing inspiration for the building of churches that honestly reflect and serve the meaning and purpose of the Eucharist, of God's dwelling with his people. To achieve this at the present time the Pope asks that attention be "given to the norms regarding the construction and décor of sacred buildings" (*EdE* 50).

The past half century has been an ambiguous time for the building of Catholic churches. Today, when there is question of a new church in a parish, the average Catholic, with the instinct of faith, will often plead for a building "that looks like a church." A Catholic church building—in its form and structure—speaks of the supernatural and of transcendence. In its beauty, the Church evokes the mystery that it shelters. To assert, as some have, that the church becomes the house of God only through the gathered assembly is a view compatible only with a very "low" sense of eucharistic presence and prescinds from the meaning of the solemn Rite of Dedication of a Church. The challenge now is to develop a style of architecture inspired by the liturgical directives of Vatican II, much as the baroque was inspired by the reforms of the Council of Trent.

The church building and decoration should speak of the intensity of God's presence in the Eucharist and the sacraments and point to the kingdom of God that is both present and still to come. "The house of prayer must be expressive of the presence of God and suited for the Sacrifice of Christ as well as reflective of the community that celebrates there" (National Council of Catholic Bishops, *Built of Living Stones*, c. 1). "A church that simply blends into the environing culture and society, adopting its perspectives, values and language, is dysfunctional" (Robert Barron, "Beyond Beige Churches." *Antiphon*, 6, no. 3, 2001, 20).

According to the Second Vatican Council's Constitution on the Liturgy and the postconciliar Rite of Dedication of a Church and an Altar, the Church herself, the living temple of God, is "symbolized in places of worship built of stone," so that the church building is a "visible sign of the living Church, God's building that is formed of the people themselves. The church building is meant to reflect the mystery of the Church, which is the communion of God and humanity wrought through the paschal mystery of Christ's death and resurrection and ascension" (Timothy Vaverek, "The Church Building and Participation in the Paschal Mystery." *Sacred Architecture* [Spring 2001], 11). The church is the place where the faithful celebrate the liturgical rites, of which the Mass is the supreme expression, as a means of deepening their participation in the paschal mystery which those rites signify and make present. A Catholic church building is a sacred space that reflects how the Church understands herself, and this self-understanding is essentially expressed in the sacramental and hierarchical arrangement of the altar, the crucifix, the tabernacle, the place for proclaiming the Word, the images of Christ and the saints, and the seating for priests and congregation. It is such a building the Holy Father envisages when he calls for attention "to be given to the norms regulating the construction and décor of sacred buildings" (*EdE* 50). In his ideal for the church building, "the cathedrals, the humble country churches, the religious music, architecture, sculpture and painting all irradiate the mystery of the *verum Corpus natum de Maria Virgine* towards which everything converges in a movement of wonder" (*EdE* 50).

"A Treasure Greater Than Those of Any Other Art" (*CCC* 1156)

Music expresses and nurtures the Church's faith in the mystery of the Eucharist. The Holy Father's concern in the encyclical extends to sacred music, of which he singles out "the inspired Gregorian melodies" (*EdE* 49) and the masterpieces of great composers.

These are part of the artistic culture that has grown up around the liturgy of the Eucharist. The Second Vatican Council's Constitution on the Liturgy affirmed the preeminence of sacred music as "a necessary or integral part of the solemn liturgy" (*Sacrosanctum Concilium* 112). It "is to be considered the more holy, the more closely connected it is with the liturgical action" because its purpose is "the glory of God and the sanctification of the faithful" (ibid.).

The Council requested that the Church's "treasury of sacred music be preserved and cultivated with great care" (ibid., 114). "The whole body of the faithful" are to be enabled "to contribute that active participation which is rightly theirs" by "religious singing" (ibid., 118). "Gregorian chant" is to "be given pride of place in liturgical services" (ibid., 116). "Other kinds of sacred music, especially polyphony" are to be given a place "as long as they accord with the spirit of the liturgical action" (ibid., 116). "The pipe organ is to be held in high esteem … for it is the traditional musical instrument …. Other instruments may also be admitted for use in divine worship … on condition they are suitable or can be made suitable for sacred use and that they accord with the dignity of the temple" (ibid., 120). "Composers, animated by the Christian spirit," are encouraged "to produce compositions which have the qualities proper to genuine sacred music" (ibid., 121).

In the forty years since the Constitution on the Liturgy was promulgated, music has become part of the Mass in the average Catholic parish to an unprecedented degree. More resources of personnel and money are being devoted to it and new compositions proliferate. There are many choirs and singing groups and instrumentalists who put themselves at the service of the liturgy. Yet to the extent to which music has been restricted to what all can play or sing, the tradition of chant and polyphony has become unavailable. The instructions of the Council are not easily reconciled with themselves.

Within a short time after the Council, some great choirs were disbanded and secular forms of music were introduced into the Mass. Today, ballads and popular music of various kinds predominate in many parishes; the organ has difficulty competing with guitars and other instruments; the Gregorian chant has been generally banished along with Latin texts. There is, as well, the need to integrate appropriate music from different cultures. Music there is in abundance, but all too often not music that speaks of the glory and transcendent holiness of God or that fosters a sense of adoration and reverence towards the eucharistic sacrifice or the Blessed Sacrament. Nor does much of this music express adequately the liturgy as action of the Church in the way the Church envisages, "with the ministers in each degree fulfilling their ministry and the people participating in it"

(*Musicam Sacram* 21). "The mystery of the liturgy with its hierarchical and community nature" (ibid.) has to be manifested in a way that says something about the nature of the Church herself.

The situation worldwide is such that, in an address at a public audience in February of this year, the Holy Father appealed for "an examination of conscience so that the beauty of music and singing may continually return to the liturgy. Worship should be purified from stylistic rough edges, sloppy expression and texts poorly in keeping with the greatness of the action being celebrated" (*L'Osservatore Romano*, 26 Feb. 2003). Music shall foster participation and piety, but these are culturally conditioned. The concern is universal; the solution yet to be achieved.

TOWARDS RETRIEVAL

The conclusion towards which this chapter of the encyclical leads is the Holy Father's urgent appeal, especially to priests, to undertake on behalf of the whole Church a return to the Church's great liturgical tradition and the form in which it is expressed as a means of giving full value to the mystery of the Eucharist (cf. *EdE* 52). In the truth and goodness that are the essence of eucharistic ritual may be found the beauty that does not fade nor deceive and that can awaken in artists the will to let their skill serve the mystery.

The beauty of Christ's presence and action in the Eucharist reaffirms the goodness of humanity and will awaken in believers amazement and wonder at the extravagance in the gift of the Eucharist of him who is Creator, Savior and life-giving Spirit.

LIKE THE WOMAN WHO ANOINTED JESUS IN BETHANY,
THE CHURCH HAS FEARED NO "EXTRAVAGANCE,"
DEVOTING THE BEST OF HER RESOURCES
TO EXPRESSING HER WONDER AND ADORATION
BEFORE THE UNSURPASSABLE GIFT OF THE EUCHARIST.
NO LESS THAN THE FIRST DISCIPLES CHARGED WITH
PREPARING THE "LARGE UPPER ROOM,"
SHE HAS FELT THE NEED, DOWN THE CENTURIES
AND IN HER ENCOUNTERS WITH DIFFERENT CULTURES,
TO CELEBRATE THE EUCHARIST IN
A SETTING WORTHY OF SO GREAT A MYSTERY.
IN THE WAKE OF JESUS' OWN WORDS AND ACTIONS,
AND BUILDING UPON THE RITUAL HERITAGE OF JUDAISM,
THE CHRISTIAN LITURGY WAS BORN.

Ecclesia de Eucharistia (48)

Michelangelo's dome towers over Bernini's Baldachino in the Patriarchal Basilica of St. Peter.

WE NOW ANOINT THIS ALTAR.
MAY GOD IN HIS POWER MAKE IT HOLY, A VISIBLE SIGN OF THE MYSTERY OF CHRIST,
WHO OFFERED HIMSELF FOR THE LIFE OF THE WORLD.

Anointing of the Altar, Rite of Dedication of an Altar

Wherever this gospel is proclaimed in the whole world, what she has done will be spoken of in memory of her (cf. *Mk* 14-19).
Top left: The Pope in Spain, 1982. Top right: The Pope at the Church of the Holy Sepulcher in Jerusalem, 2000. The Holy
Father kisses the stone on which tradition says the body of Christ was washed and anointed for burial. Bottom: Anointing
an altar in Africa, 1984. Opposite: The Pope amid Rococo splendor in Switzerland, 1984.

LORD, MAY OUR PRAYERS ASCEND AS INCENSE IN YOUR SIGHT.
AS THIS BUILDING IS FILLED WITH FRAGRANCE SO MAY YOUR CHURCH
FILL THE WORLD WITH THE FRAGRANCE OF CHRIST.

Incensation of the Altar, Rite of Dedication of an Altar

Zeal for your house consumes me: Top left: the Pope at Mass in his private chapel, 2002. Top right: Croatia, 1994.
Bottom left: Gaudi's Cathedral in Spain, 1982. Bottom right: St. Paul Outside the Walls, Rome, 2000.

IT CAN BE SAID THAT THE EUCHARIST,
WHILE SHAPING THE CHURCH AND HER SPIRITUALITY,
HAS ALSO POWERFULLY AFFECTED "CULTURE"
AND THE ARTS IN PARTICULAR.

Ecclesia de Eucharistia (49)

The United States, 1987.

Top left: The Holy Father surrounded by Byzantine frescoes in Ukraine, 2001. Top right: Africa, 1995. Bottom left: Ivory Coast, 1990. Bottom right: Huambo, 1992. Opposite: Beneath Michelangelo's *Last Judgment* in the Sistine Chapel, 1994.

How lovely is your dwelling place, O LORD of hosts!
My soul longs, indeed it faints for the courts of the LORD;
My heart and my flesh sing for joy to the living God.

Ps 84: 1–2

Top: The Pope and modernity in Malta, 1990. Bottom: Africa, 1995. Opposite: Stained glass in Brazil, 1997.

IN MY NUMEROUS PASTORAL VISITS
I HAVE SEEN, THROUGHOUT THE WORLD,
THE GREAT VITALITY WHICH THE CELEBRATION OF THE EUCHARIST
CAN HAVE WHEN MARKED BY THE FORMS,
STYLES AND SENSIBILITIES OF DIFFERENT CULTURES.
BY ADAPTATION TO THE CHANGING CONDITIONS OF TIME AND PLACE,
THE EUCHARIST OFFERS SUSTENANCE NOT ONLY
TO INDIVIDUALS BUT TO ENTIRE PEOPLES,
AND IT SHAPES CULTURES INSPIRED BY CHRISTIANITY.

Ecclesia de Eucharistia (51)

Faith and culture. A chalice made from an African carving, 1995.

Hosanna in the Highest!
Blessed is he who comes in the name of the Lord!

Pilgrim Pope. Top: The Pope greets crowds from an open car in Africa, 1982. Bottom: A shower of confetti in Brazil, 1980.

Our Gospel did not come to you in word alone (cf. *1 Th* 1:5). Top left: Riding across a carpet of flowers in Guatemala, 1983. Top right: In Mexico, 1990. Bottom: Reaching out to a Bennin Paraku horseman in 1993. Opposite: The Holy Father at an outdoor altar in the Philippines, 1981.

APPROACH [THIS ALTAR] WITH THE LOVE OF GOD AND WITH FAITH.
BLESSED IS HE WHO COMES IN THE NAME OF THE LORD;
GOD IS THE LORD, AND HAS APPEARED AMONG US.

Liturgy of St. John Chrysostom

Top: Receiving gifts at the altar in Ukraine, 1988. Bottom: Greeting natives in the South Pacific, 1984.
Opposite: India, 1986.

Top left: Peering through an airplane window on the trip to Ireland, 1979. Top right: Making a joyful noise in Africa, 1995. Bottom left: Wearing a Native American chasuble in the United States, 1987. Bottom right: Gifts for the altar in the Philippines, 1995

HOLY, HOLY, HOLY LORD SABAOTH,
HEAVEN AND EARTH ARE FULL OF YOUR GLORY! HEAVEN IS FULL,
AND FULL IS THE EARTH WITH YOUR MAGNIFICENT GLORY,
LORD OF VIRTUES. FULL ALSO IS THIS SACRIFICE, WITH YOUR STRENGTH AND
YOUR COMMUNION; FOR TO YOU WE OFFER THIS LIVING SACRIFICE,
THIS UNBLOODY OBLATION.

Sacramentary of Serapion

Evocative of the Gospels' narrative of Christ's entry into Jerusalem, children climb trees to view the Pope in Cuba, 1998.
Next page: The Holy Father greets tribesmen in the South Pacific, 1984.

Top: Amazonians gather around the Holy Father at Castel Gandolfo, 2002. Bottom: The Pope venerates the shrine of a Korean saint, 1984.

Ave Crux, spes unica! We hail you, O holy cross!
You bring us the One who twenty centuries ago was acclaimed
in Jerusalem by other young people and by the crowd:
"Blessed is he who comes in the name of the Lord."
We all join in this song, repeating:
Blessed is he who comes in the name of the Lord!
Yes! Blessed are you, O Christ, who also comes to us today
with your message of love and life. And blessed is your holy cross,
from which flows the salvation of the world yesterday,
today and forever. Ave Crux! Praised be Jesus Christ.

Pope John Paul II, Palm Sunday, 1998

CHAPTER SIX

TOGETHER AT THE TABLE WITH MARY OUR MODEL OF PRAISE AND THANKSGIVING

Reverend Monsignor Michael J. Bransfield, M Div

My Soul magnifies the Lord,

and my spirit rejoices in God my Savior,

for he has regarded the low estate of his handmaiden.

For behold, henceforth all generations will call me blessed;

for he who is mighty has done great things for me and holy is his name. *-Lk 1:46-49*

Imagine her immeasurable joy, her wonder, her ecstatic expectation in the face of all that God had now begun to accomplish in her and through her. And all because she had the courage to say yes. Mary, the handmaiden of the Lord, the Mother of Jesus, provides for us in every place and for all time, the perfect response to the call of God and the promptings of his Holy Spirit. Indeed, generations past and generations to come will call her blessed. For in trusting, she overcame fear and anxiety; because of her unconditional assent, she gave birth to Hope and the promise of a new beginning for all humankind.

A century ago, Catholics of the United States sought to memorialize this woman of great faith and her timeless example with the establishment of a monumental church in their nation's capital city. Overcoming the obstacles brought on by a world war, a Great Depression, and yet another world war, Catholics of every ancestry, age and economic background ultimately succeeded in creating the "Great Hymn in Stone" that, in our day and time, is known as the Basilica of the National Shrine of the Immaculate Conception. Writing from the vantage point of Rector of this magnificent sanctuary of prayer and pilgrimage, I am constantly struck by the relevancy of Mary and her model of faith in the everyday lives of Catholic men, women and our young people. Though forms of devotion and piety have changed over time, Mary's role in the chronicle of salvation history remains a compelling and model response in the context of difficult and conflicting life choices. Because she was and is the central figure in the revelation of the New and Everlasting Covenant of God's love, Mary—more than any other—points the way to true Christian discipleship. Her singular response in the face of incredulous and daunting circumstance makes possible our assent, our trust in the One who comes to us where we are and who takes us to places we never imagined.

MICHAEL J. BRANSFIELD has been associated with the Basilica of the National Shrine of the Immaculate Conception since 1980 when he was appointed the Shrine's Assistant Director. When the Shrine was designated a Basilica in 1990, Monsignor Bransfield became the Shrine's first rector. Named a Prelate of Honor by the Holy Father in 1987, Monsignor Bransfield serves on several boards including that of The Catholic University of America.

In his encyclical, *Ecclesia de Eucharista*, His Holiness Pope John Paul II asserts Mary's rightful place in our eucharistic celebration. As a people confronted with competing demands and distractions that would lead us from the fundamental truth of human existence, it is incumbent on the followers of Jesus to seek out the all-encompassing Truth that alone is capable of dispelling the illusions that surround us. There and only there—at the Table of the Lord, in the Eucharist of his body and blood—do we experience the light that pierces the darkness of fear and despair that daily confronts us. It is there, in the context of a shared and sacred meal that has bound Christians together since they first did so "in memory of him," that our focus is sharpened, our anxieties quelled, our hope renewed. And it is there, in the supportive, faith-filled embrace of others, that we have the courage to say yes—like Mary—to who we are and all that we are asked to become by the same loving and assuring Father.

The mystery that Christians have celebrated for over two-thousand years is the incomprehensible love of the Creator for his children, made manifest in the incarnation of his very own Son. Through the Eucharist, we affirm our faith in and acceptance of this central belief of Christian faith. In so doing, we assert that, in fact, we are in this world, but not of it (*Jn* 15:19), called out by God to claim our true identity as children of God and yet called forth to engage this same world, all the while bearing witness to the gift we have received in abundance. Like Mary, we are asked to bear Christ to the world. Like her, we are asked to reveal the presence of God's will active among us—changing us and redirecting us to our sanctified destiny, if only we also have the courage to say *yes*.

MY SPIRIT REJOICES IN GOD MY SAVIOR

In his encyclical, the Holy Father offers a potent allegory of Mary's capacity even now to inspire a greater appreciation for the Eucharist: "Mary also anticipated, in the mystery of the incarnation, the Church's eucharistic faith. When at the Visitation she bore in her womb the Word made flesh, she became in some way a "tabernacle"—the first "tabernacle" in history—in which the Son of God, still invisible to our human gaze, allowed himself to be adored by Elizabeth, radiating his light as it were through the eyes and the voice of Mary" (*Ecclesia de Eucharistia* 55). Similarly, we who have likewise answered yes to God's invitation must also reveal Christ who is truly in us. Others must see through our words and actions something extraordinary—something not of this world—something that gives pause to reconsider life's purpose, something that is utterly transforming. Indeed, they must see Christ and through us feel his power to forgive, to empathize, to gently guide and ultimately to reconcile human interaction and activity with humanity's sanctified purpose and destiny. As the National Conference of Catholic Bishops' 1973 Pastoral Letter on Mary makes clear: "Through her life of faith on earth, and now through her union with the risen Christ, the Mother of Jesus is the supreme example of loving association with the Savior in his mission of redeeming mankind" (*Behold Your Mother: Woman of Faith* 66).

Now as then, Mary provides for us the primordial answer to the invitation—to the reality of God's love made manifest in the incarnation of his Son Jesus—"Let it be done to me according to your word" (*Lk* 1:38). It is at the Eucharist that Mary and her relevance to our Faith is most apparent. She, who first allowed the Gift of God's great love and mercy to take root in her life, guides us and encourages us to do the same. In our yes we are linked to Mary and are able to embrace more deeply the mystery that the Eucharist reveals—God living among us: consoling, forgiving and healing a troubled world in us and through us. "[T]here is a profound analogy between the fiat which Mary said in reply to the angel and the 'amen' which every believer says when receiving the body of the Lord. Mary was asked to believe that the One whom she conceived 'through the Holy Spirit' was 'the Son of God' (*Lk* 1:30-35). In continuity with the Virgin's faith, in the eucharistic mystery we are asked to believe that the same Jesus Christ, Son of God and Son of Mary, becomes present in his full humanity and divinity under the signs of bread and wine" (*EdE* 55).

Every generation will call me blessed

Throughout the Basilica of the National Shrine of the Immaculate Conception there are more than sixty chapels and oratories dedicated to Mary and her intercession through time as experienced among generations of diverse cultures. Each summarizes a particular culture's reverence throughout its history for her role in the revelation of God's love, and each bears witness to her preeminent place in the life and ministry of the Church. Mary, as the central theme of these many chapels and oratories, provides the unifying response to the invitation and the call we experience in the Eucharist, a response that transcends ethnic and cultural distinction. As pilgrims from near and far gather within these marvelously adorned mosaic spaces to contemplate their own "journey of Christian living," they cannot help but also contemplate this marvelous woman who even now points the way to her Son. Whether in the Chapel of Our Lady of Hostyn; Our Lady Queen of Peace; Our Mother of Africa; Our Lady of Lourdes; or the Chapel of Our Lady of Good Health, Vailankanni, Mary is our reference point as we come to the Table of the Lord. Her *Magnificat*—her prayer of thanksgiving and praise—foreshadows the basis for our Eucharist, our joyful expression of thanksgiving to God. With her, our souls "magnify the Lord," our spirits "rejoice in God our Savior." Pope John Paul II further emphasizes the link between Mary's response to having been chosen by God and the response asked of us in the eucharistic liturgy. The Holy Father explains: "The Magnificat expresses Mary's spirituality, and there is nothing greater than this spirituality for helping us to experience the mystery of the Eucharist. The Eucharist has been given to us so that our life, like that of Mary, may become a complete Magnificat!" (*EdE* 58).

Too often, and for too long, Catholics' emphasis on Mary has been a cause for division among Christians of varying denominations. Intense debate has centered on the proportionality of Marian devotion; on the legitimacy of articles of Catholic faith such as the Dogma of the Immaculate Conception; and on the frequency of Marian references in the Church's liturgical cycle of festivals and solemn celebrations. And yet we have abundant evidence in Holy Scripture and in Tradition that Christians from earliest days extolled Mary as the perfect example of trust, obedience and abiding faithfulness to God and his Son Jesus. Our ancestors in faith recognized Mary as the central figure at the beginning and at the end of the life and ministry of her Son Jesus. From her lips at the wedding feast of Cana—at the very outset of her Son's earthly ministry—we gain our clearest instruction for true discipleship: "Do whatever he tells you" (*Jn* 2:5). And from the cross, in the culmination of his ministry, Christ gives to the Church his mother as its own: "Behold your mother" (*Jn* 19:27). It is at this moment when Mary's dual nature as both disciple and Mother of the Church is revealed. She is there in the final agonizing moments of her Son's life as undaunted follower and loving mother. She is faithful in once again accepting the will of the Father when every natural inclination would be to resist the circumstances before her. Again, Mary gives her Son to others—to us—in a final act of abandonment to the reality far bigger than the conflicting emotions that surely enveloped her. Again, Mary summons the courage to say *yes*.

For he who is mighty has done great things for me

It is right and fitting that the Church hold up Mary to the faithful and to the world as the perfect role model—as the one who, better than any other, points the way on our life's pilgrimage toward true happiness and lasting fulfillment. Even as secular culture designates film stars, sports heroes and titans of business as role models in the pursuit of idealized notions of success and happiness, we the Church must have the courage to proclaim Mary and her witness—her humility, faithfulness and obedience—as our model of what is possible when we open ourselves to the power of God's great and unconditional love.

Contemplating as we must Mary's profound expression of praise and thanksgiving—her Magnificat—at all that God had made possible in her life, we will be truly prepared to gather at the Table of the Lord with minds and hearts open to the Father's will. With her, we assent to the possibility—the likelihood—that God will transform us and use us to accomplish his redemptive work in a troubled and desperate world. In our own

praise and thanksgiving, we, like Mary, receive Christ not as our possession but as our Gift to be given generously to others who likewise seek healing and hope, consolation and love—the possibility of a new beginning.
Returning again to the Holy Father's pastoral insight and guidance we are encouraged to "listen to Mary most
holy … in whom the mystery of the Eucharist appears more than in anyone else as a mystery of light. Gazing
upon Mary, we come to know the transforming power present in the Eucharist. In her we see the world
renewed in love" (*EdE* 62).

As a people who have seen with our own eyes and come to know in our own hearts the beauty and
power of God's great love, let us magnify the Lord in our day and time. With spirits enlivened by all that the
Father has made possible, let us together rejoice in God our Savior. Claiming the promise made known again
and again at his Eucharist, let us proclaim his boundless love and mercy now and for generations yet to come.
"Holy is his name."

IF WE WISH TO REDISCOVER
IN ALL ITS RICHNESS
THE PROFOUND RELATIONSHIP BETWEEN
THE CHURCH AND THE EUCHARIST,
WE CANNOT NEGLECT MARY,
MOTHER AND MODEL OF THE CHURCH.

Ecclesia de Eucharistia (53)

Woman of the Eucharist. The Pope leads a eucharistic procession at Lourdes, France, holding a monstrance as he rides past the basilica, 1983.

YOU, THEOTOKOS, ARE THE CENSER OF GOLD AND PERFUME
GIVING FORTH THE HOLY FRAGRANCE OF CHRIST.

Byzantine Liturgy

Mother of God. The Pope venerates Mary around the world. Top left: Cuba, 1998. Top right: United States, 1995.
Bottom: The Patriarchal Basilica, 1987. Opposite: At Lourdes, the Holy Father venerates the site of the apparition of
the Virgin Mary to St. Bernadette in 1858.

BUT IN ADDITION TO HER SHARING
IN THE EUCHARISTIC BANQUET,
AN INDIRECT PICTURE OF MARY'S RELATIONSHIP
WITH THE EUCHARIST CAN BE HAD,
BEGINNING WITH HER INTERIOR DISPOSITION.
MARY IS A "*WOMAN OF THE EUCHARIST*"
IN HER WHOLE LIFE. THE CHURCH,
WHICH LOOKS TO MARY AS A MODEL,
IS ALSO CALLED TO IMITATE
HER IN HER RELATIONSHIP WITH THIS
MOST HOLY MYSTERY.

Ecclesia de Eucharistia (53)

Presenting a Rosary to a statue of the Virgin in Colombia, 1986. Opposite: Latin America, 1996.

YOU WERE THE FIRST TO BELIEVE.
YOU PERSEVERED IN PRAYER WITH THE DISCIPLES IN THE UPPER ROOM.
YOU WERE A UNIQUE WITNESS TO THE MYSTERY OF JESUS.
ALL GENERATIONS HAVE CALLED YOU BLESSED.
NOW THE CHURCH LOOKS YET AGAIN TO YOU FOR INSPIRATION AND HELP.

Pope John Paul II, Marian Prayer Day by Day (Prayer for Wednesday)

Top left: Candles and flowers before the Madonna in Benelux, 1985. Top right: Venerating the site of the Annunciation at Nazareth, 2000. Bottom: At the Church of the Nativity in Bethlehem, 2000. The Pope reflects upon the mystery of the incarnation.

✠

GABRIEL BEHELD IN AMAZEMENT, O MOTHER OF GOD,
YOUR HOLINESS AND YOUR PURITY'S SPLENDOR; AND HE CRIED TO YOU:
"HOW SHALL I GREET YOU? HOW SHALL I ADDRESS YOU? I AM HESITANT; I MARVEL!
BUT, AS I WAS COMMANDED, I SHALL GREET YOU: HAIL, FULL OF GRACE!"
Prayer Tín Oraiótita, Akathist Hymn

The Queen is arrayed in gold. The Pope venerates the miraculous icon of Our Lady of Czestochowa in Poland, 1999.
As the bush was burning but not consumed, so did you give birth while yet a virgin. Next page: The Patriarchal Basilica
ablaze in joy as Mary's Holy Year is inaugurated, August, 1987.

HAIL, JESUS, SON OF MARY, IN THE SACRED HOST YOU ARE THE TRUE GOD.

Pope John Paul II, 19th International Marian Congress, August 15, 1996

Slovenia, 1996.

MARY, THROUGHOUT HER LIFE AT CHRIST'S SIDE
AND NOT ONLY ON CALVARY, MADE HER OWN
THE SACRIFICIAL DIMENSION OF THE EUCHARIST.
WHEN SHE BROUGHT THE CHILD JESUS TO THE TEMPLE
IN JERUSALEM "TO PRESENT HIM TO THE LORD" (*LK* 2:22),
SHE HEARD THE AGED SIMEON ANNOUNCE THAT
THE CHILD WOULD BE A "SIGN OF CONTRADICTION"
AND THAT A SWORD WOULD ALSO PIERCE
HER OWN HEART (CF. *LK* 2:34-35).
THE TRAGEDY OF HER SON'S CRUCIFIXION WAS THUS FORETOLD,
AND IN SOME SENSE MARY'S STABAT MATER
AT THE FOOT OF THE CROSS WAS FORESHADOWED.
IN HER DAILY PREPARATION FOR CALVARY,
MARY EXPERIENCED A KIND OF 'ANTICIPATED EUCHARIST'
—ONE MIGHT SAY A "SPIRITUAL COMMUNION"—
OF DESIRE AND OF OBLATION, WHICH WOULD CULMINATE IN
HER UNION WITH HER SON IN HIS PASSION, AND THEN
FIND EXPRESSION AFTER EASTER BY HER PARTAKING
IN THE EUCHARIST WHICH THE APOSTLES
CELEBRATED AS THE MEMORIAL OF THAT PASSION.

Ecclesia de Eucharistia (56)

The mosaic of Mary, *Mater Ecclesiae*, can be seen from St. Peter's Square. It bears the Holy Father's coat of arms and motto.

Is there one who would not weep Whelmed in misery so deep;
Christ's dear mother to behold?

Stabat Mater

All his bitter anguish sharing. Top left: The Pope venerates an icon of the Mother of Perpetual Help, Ukraine, 1988.
Top right: The Holy Father contemplates the *Pieta* in the Vatican Basilica before each Mass he celebrates there.
Bottom left: In India, 1986. Bottom right: In Croatia, 1998. Opposite: The statue of Our Lady of Fatima before a vast crowd
gathered to see the Pope in Portugal, 1982. The bullet that nearly took the Pope's life the previous year is set into the
statue's crown. Next page: The Pope leads a procession in honor of Mary at St. Mary Major in Rome, 1988.

Top left: Zaire, 1985. Top right: Salus Populi Romani icon in Rome, 1987. Bottom: On the altar in Peru, 1985.

O MOTHER, YOU KNOW THE SUFFERINGS
AND HOPES OF THE CHURCH AND THE WORLD:
COME TO THE AID OF YOUR CHILDREN IN THE DAILY TRIALS
WHICH LIFE BRINGS TO EACH ONE,
AND GRANT THAT, THANKS TO THE EFFORTS OF ALL,
THE DARKNESS WILL NOT PREVAIL OVER THE LIGHT.
TO YOU, DAWN OF SALVATION, WE COMMIT
OUR JOURNEY THROUGH THE NEW MILLENNIUM,
SO THAT WITH YOU AS GUIDE
ALL PEOPLE MAY KNOW CHRIST,
THE LIGHT OF THE WORLD AND ITS ONLY SAVIOR,
WHO REIGNS WITH THE FATHER AND THE HOLY SPIRIT
FOR EVER AND EVER. AMEN.

Pope John Paul II, Act of Entrustment to the Virgin Mary, October 8, 2000

CONCLUSION

INTO THE DEEP:
CONCLUSION OF ECCLESIA DE EUCHARISTIA

Most Reverend John J. Myers, JCD

After setting forth in this magnificent encyclical the Church's profound faith in the Eucharist, Pope John Paul II allows himself, in his conclusions, a brief personal note: the encyclical is published during the twenty-fifth year of his Petrine ministry. During a half-century of offering Holy Mass, as he relates, his eyes have gazed on the Host and the Chalice, recognizing in the consecrated bread and wine the Lord and Savior who opens our eyes to light and our hearts to hope.

How could it be otherwise for a man who has spent his entire papal ministry traveling from country to country, evangelizing the world in the process? How could it be otherwise for a man who clearly trusts in Divine Providence, in the role the Lord of History has assigned to him in preaching the gospel? Only by recognizing the constant accompaniment of Christ Jesus in the Eucharist would one have the courage to undertake the kind of far-flung apostolic mission that has been the hallmark of the Pontificate of Pope John Paul II. St. Athanasius has written, "When together we are nourished [by Christ's body and blood] we truly celebrate his paschal mystery" (*Epistolae paschales* 4). It is this vision, that of the community of the universal Church gathering in anticipation of the banquet feast of heaven, that the Pope both fosters and celebrates with his apostolic journeys.

The Holy Father comments that in the consecrated bread and wine, time and space "merge" and the drama of Golgotha is re-presented in a living way, thereby revealing its mysterious "contemporaneity." The Pope here faithfully transmits the ancient teaching: the Eucharist is contemporaneous because every offering of the mystery is always an *anamnesis* (i.e., it is not simply the recollection of a past event, but the celebration of Christ's eternal paschal sacrifice now efficaciously actualized). Each day, he says, his faith has recognized in the consecrated bread and wine the Risen Lord who touches minds and hearts. There the Holy Father, together with all bishops and priests, together with all Catholics, stands with Christ the High Priest, the one Mediator, who continually celebrates the paschal liturgy, overcoming sin and death and imparting to us his own Divine Life.

MOST REVEREND JOHN J. MYERS is Archbishop of Newark and Vice-President of the Pope John Paul II Cultural Center. He has participated extensively in numerous Canon Law projects and holds a JCD Doctorate in Canonical Jurisprudence. He has produced scholarly writings on a range of topics, including diocesan finance, ecclesial ministries, the rights of unborn children and the family.

As so often during the course of his papacy, and in accord with Christ's command to Peter to "feed my sheep," the Holy Father writes in order to strengthen the eucharistic faith of all the members of the Church. He invokes the beautiful fourteenth-century hymn, often sung at Benediction, and the inspiration for so many composers over the centuries: *Ave verum corpus natum de Maria Virgine, vere passum, immolatum, in cruce pro homine!* "Hail true body born of the Virgin Mary, truly suffered and sacrificed on the cross for our sakes!" How great the gift of the Eucharist! How great the treasure that Christ has imparted to his Church! Indeed, the Pope calls the Eucharist the "heart of the world" for which "each man and woman, even unconsciously, yearns."

Gift and givenness

It is no surprise that, as a former professor of philosophy, with a specialty in the field known as phenomenology, Pope John Paul II creatively reflects on the Holy Eucharist from a perspective highlighting certain contemporary phenomenological themes, in particular the notions of gift and givenness. The gift, it is argued, when taken in its true and unfettered givenness, cannot be bound by pre-determining conditions. Its presence must be allowed to appear without delimiting qualifications if we are to see it, not as tailored to our own horizons, our own pre-conceptions, but rather in its own uniqueness and difference.

The Pope calls our attention to the Eucharist as precisely the kind of gift and presence that must be allowed to appear in its fullness. We cannot see the Eucharist simply bound to our normal conditions of subjectivity. The Holy Father asks us to see this sacrament as it truly is, as the unfathomable gift of God, as a transcendent mystery, as an extraordinary phenomenon of God's abundant goodness and grace that transgresses the natural order of our expectations, exploding the reductive, pragmatic tendencies inherent in our everyday, anticipatory determinations. The Eucharist is the greatest "form" mediating God's presence among us. Therefore, it must be allowed to appear and subsist in its authentic integrity as the gift beyond human understanding. This is why the Pope incisively says that this mystery "taxes our mind's ability to pass beyond appearances." For it is precisely the reduction to the ordinary, the everyday, the unimaginative, the instrumental, that will cause the uniqueness of the gift to remain hidden from us.

St. Thomas Aquinas, the great theologian of the Church, knew that the gift of the Eucharist would be masked and obscured if judged not by transcendent and spiritual horizons, by the mysteries of God's own life, but by our everyday, ordinary, merely sensible range. This is why the Pope immediately cites St. Thomas' great hymn, *Adoro Te Devote*: "seeing, touching, tasting are in you deceived"—deceived, of course, because only the light of faith allows us to surpass the ordinariness of the senses and to see the gift in its unalloyed luminosity. This is why the Holy Father teaches, as well, that the Eucharist in the plenitude of its complex and multivalent meaning—as communion, sacrifice, presence and banquet—cannot allow for reduction or exploitation. To do so would do violence to the unique gift itself, to misunderstand it, to exchange its supernatural and polysemous meanings for the porridge of mere ideology. Forms of our own making cannot bind the gift and mystery that is the Eucharist; Christ's sacramental presence can only be adored in wonder and gratitude.

Put out into the deep water and lower your nets for a catch (*Lk* 5:4)

The Church draws her strength—her evangelizing mission, her commitment to holiness, her thirst for justice, her apostolic spirit—from Christ's presence in the Eucharist. The Pope notes again, as he so often has during his pontificate, that the Church begins a new age at the dawn of this third millennium. It is a fresh, hopeful, joyful start, even while it is in full continuity with the life of the Church in ages past. All desire for reform and renewal, then, both in our personal lives and in the Church itself, should be centered in Christ.

The Holy Father makes clear that it is not a matter of finding some "new program." There is no need for an "ecclesiogenesis," as if the Church could be remodeled according to contemporary fashions and tastes. Rather, the Church has been established by Christ; its charter may be found in the Gospel and the living

Tradition. And at the center of both Scripture and Tradition is Christ's unique gift of the Eucharist. It is for this reason that the Pope makes clear that any plan for the spiritual renewal of the Church, for the spiritual renewal of our own lives, necessarily "passes through the Eucharist."

Pope John Paul II had argued, when teaching philosophy earlier in his life, that atheism, whether rooted in Marxism or existentialism, is ultimately solipsistic, unable to achieve a proper notion of intersubjectivity, of authentic interchange among men and women. The Eucharist, on the other hand, by sacramentally manifesting the presence of God, draws us toward deeper humanizing and self-transcending relationships with both God and each other. It signals presence amidst absence, joy amidst suffering; it allows us, as we say at Mass, to live in "joyful hope" until Christ comes again.

The Eucharist reminds us that the Word of God who became incarnate, suffered, died for us and rose from the dead, offers himself in the form of humble elements, his flesh and blood for the life of the world. As the Lord himself has promised, "Unlike your ancestors who ate bread in the desert and died, who eats of this bread will live forever" (*Jn* 6, 49-51). It is not surprising, then, that the *Catechism* of the Council of Trent called the Eucharist the "fountain of all graces," containing as it does the Author of all the Sacraments, Christ our Lord (*Catechism of the Council of Trent* [Trans. by John McHugh and Charles Callan. New York: Joseph Wagner, 1954] 242).

THAT THEY MAY BE ONE

The Holy Father is also quick to note in his conclusions that the Church of the third millennium retains a firm and unyielding commitment to ecumenism. Already he has written on this theme at great length, confirming the Church's profound concern for the reunion of all Christians, in such significant documents as the encyclical *Ut unum sint* and in his approval of the Joint Declaration on Justification. The Pope notes that, despite obstacles, the Church's indefeasible goal is the sharing of the one Eucharist by all those who share one baptism in Christ. This goal has been clearly strengthened by decades of theological research dedicated to the eucharistic mystery.

Achieving complete unity of faith and communion is a telos that the Catholic Church, along with other churches and ecclesial communities, longs for and cherishes. The Holy Father makes clear, however, that in our worthy desire to achieve the union of all Christians, we cannot obscure the unique gift and treasure that is the Holy Eucharist, nor may we engage in what the Second Vatican Council called a "false irenicism." For this treasure is inextricably linked with the episcopal and presbyterial ministries of Holy Orders, along with the Church's understanding of legitimate apostolic succession. The authentic integrity of the eucharistic gift, therefore, demands that we respect the *depositum fidei* in its entirety.

Continuous solicitude for this gift and mystery of faith is essential because, as Aquinas made clear: "In this sacrament is recapitulated the whole mystery of our salvation" (*Summa theologiae III*, q. 83, a. 4, c.). Yet, it is this Eucharist itself, Christ uniquely present among us, which inexorably impels us to pursue—with unbounded hope and with complete confidence in the presence of the Holy Spirit—the goal of full communion with our separated brethren.

SCHOOL OF THE SAINTS

The Pope then calls our attention to the "school of the saints," who by their lives have been the great interpreters of the Eucharist. Saints from every nation and continent attest to the centrality of this unique sacrament. In fact, it has been one of the tasks of this pontificate to search out great witnesses to Christian holiness from every region and walk of life.

The Catholicity of the Church, and the Eucharist in its universality as God's gratuitous gift, makes all other differences among men entirely superficial. What difference does it make if men belong to different races, speak different languages, labor at different jobs, earn different wages? These distinctions are meaningless and even non-existent when gazed upon from the perspective of the gift of Christ's body and blood, poured out to redeem the sins of all men. The saints constitute a class of witnesses to the universality of the eucharistic mystery simultaneously manifesting and sealing the action of God come to fulfillment in Christ's redemptive work.

Of course, as so often during his pontificate, John Paul II invokes the Blessed Mother of God as a preeminent witness to divine action, as one in whom the eschatological pledge of the Eucharist has already come to light. Mary's Assumption represents both the proleptic anticipation and the ultimate fulfillment of Christ's final and glorious consummation of history. She also testifies to, by her simple fiat, the proper Christian acceptance of God's gifts. In her case, she quietly yet firmly accepted the providential role assigned to her by God in the mystery of salvation. In our own case, it is a matter of recognizing, gratefully but with active participation, the gift now bestowed on us in the Blessed Sacrament. In his encyclical on the role of Mary, *Mater redemptoris*, the Holy Father notes that the divine messenger says to Mary: "Do not be afraid, for you have found favor with God" (*Mater redemptoris* 9). Perhaps by an analogy of faith we can say that Christ, in the Eucharist, addresses these same words to us. Fear should be absent from our lives. The Lord has provided us with food for the journey until he comes again.

The Holy Father concludes the encyclical by noting that the Holy Eucharist, that most humble and yet most exalted of gifts, the simple grain and wine now transformed into Christ's own life—thereby uniting heaven and earth—pushes reason to its very limits. It is here that even the most profound theological reflection can only spill over into doxology and adoration. And so the Pope makes his own the words cited by Aquinas in the hymn, *Lauda, Sion*, composed for the feast of Corpus Christi: "Let us see your radiant goodness in the land of the living."

ALLOW ME, DEAR BROTHERS AND SISTERS,
TO SHARE WITH DEEP EMOTION,
AS A MEANS OF ACCOMPANYING AND STRENGTHENING YOUR FAITH,
MY OWN TESTIMONY OF FAITH IN THE MOST HOLY EUCHARIST.
Ave verum corpus natum de Maria Virgine,
vere passum, immolatum, in cruce pro homine!
HERE IS THE CHURCH'S TREASURE, THE HEART OF THE WORLD,
THE PLEDGE OF THE FULFILLMENT FOR WHICH
EACH MAN AND WOMAN, EVEN UNCONSCIOUSLY, YEARNS.
A GREAT AND TRANSCENDENT MYSTERY,
INDEED, AND ONE THAT TAXES OUR MIND'S ABILITY
TO PASS BEYOND APPEARANCES. HERE OUR SENSES FAIL US:
VISUS, TACTUS, GUSTUS IN TE FALLITUR,
IN THE WORDS OF THE HYMN *ADORO TE DEVOTE*;
YET FAITH ALONE, ROOTED IN THE WORD
OF CHRIST HANDED DOWN TO US BY THE APOSTLES,
IS SUFFICIENT FOR US. ALLOW ME, LIKE PETER AT THE END OF
THE EUCHARISTIC DISCOURSE IN JOHN'S GOSPEL,
TO SAY ONCE MORE TO CHRIST, IN THE NAME
OF THE WHOLE CHURCH AND IN THE NAME OF EACH OF YOU:
"LORD TO WHOM SHALL WE GO?
YOU HAVE THE WORDS OF ETERNAL LIFE" (*JN* 6:68).

Ecclesia de Eucharistia (59)

The Holy Father kneels at the opening of the Holy Door at Midnight Mass in the Patriarchal Basilica of St. Peter, 1999.
The opened door marked the beginning of the Holy Year 2000.

AT THE DAWN OF THIS THIRD MILLENNIUM,
WE, THE CHILDREN OF THE CHURCH, ARE CALLED TO UNDERTAKE WITH
RENEWED ENTHUSIASM THE JOURNEY OF CHRISTIAN LIVING.

Ecclesia de Eucharistia (60)

New and old. Top: A delighted pontiff sends his first email, 2001. Bottom left: The Holy Father at the newly-opened Holy Door, Christmas Eve, 1999. Bottom right: Swiss Guards at attention in traditional uniforms. Opposite: The Pope welcomes the year 2000 from his window overlooking St. Peter's Square. Next page: Jumbotron technology makes the Pope visible to everyone, even in the rain, 2000.

IN THE EUCHARIST WE HAVE JESUS,
WE HAVE HIS REDEMPTIVE SACRIFICE,
WE HAVE HIS RESURRECTION,
WE HAVE THE GIFT OF THE HOLY SPIRIT,
WE HAVE ADORATION, OBEDIENCE
AND LOVE OF THE FATHER.
WERE WE TO DISREGARD THE EUCHARIST,
HOW COULD WE OVERCOME OUR OWN DEFICIENCY?

Ecclesia de Eucharistia (60)

The Holy Father, 1993.

✦

... FOR THE SAKE OF CHRIST, WHEN I AM WEAK I AM STRONG.

2 Cor 12:10

Given for you and all. Top: Mass in Poland, 2002. Bottom: The Holy Father receives communion from Joseph Cardinal Ratzinger, Prefect, Congregation for the Doctrine of the Faith, St. Peter's Basilica, 2002.

FAITH IS NECESSARY, OR RATHER FAITH VIVIFIED BY LOVE IS NECESSARY,
TO EXPLORE THE FASCINATING DEPTH OF THIS PRESENCE OF CHRIST UNDER
THE "SIGNS" OF BREAD AND WINE. ONLY ONE WHO BELIEVES AND LOVES
CAN UNDERSTAND SOMETHING OF THE INEFFABLE MYSTERY, THANKS TO WHICH,
GOD COMES CLOSE TO OUR LITTLENESS, SEEKS OUR INFIRMITY,
REVEALS HIMSELF FOR WHAT HE IS, INFINITE SAVING LOVE.

Pope John Paul II, General Audience, June 2, 2002

Faith and love. Top: Well-wishers shout Sto lat! in honor of the Pope's 83rd birthday, May 18, 2003. Bottom left: The Pope reaches to touch hands (and hearts) in Brazil, 1980. Bottom right: "Popemobile" has entered the English lexicon and the term is synonymous with Pope John Paul II. Opposite: The Holy Father shares his paternal affection with a group of religious in Africa, 1982.

PUT OUT INTO DEEP WATER AND LOWER YOUR NETS FOR A CATCH.

Lk 5:4

Top: The Holy Father surveys the Atlantic Ocean off the coast of Brazil, 1980. Bottom: *Viva il Papa!* An exuberant crowd in the Paul VI Audience Hall greets the Pope, Vatican City, 1996.

LET US TAKE OUR PLACE, DEAR BROTHERS AND SISTERS,
AT THE SCHOOL OF THE SAINTS, WHO ARE
THE GREAT INTERPRETERS OF TRUE EUCHARISTIC PIETY.
IN THEM THE THEOLOGY OF THE EUCHARIST
TAKES ON ALL THE SPLENDOR OF A LIVED REALITY;
IT BECOMES "CONTAGIOUS" AND, IN A MANNER OF SPEAKING,
IT "WARMS OUR HEARTS." ABOVE ALL,
LET US LISTEN TO MARY MOST HOLY, IN WHOM THE MYSTERY
OF THE EUCHARIST APPEARS, MORE THAN IN ANYONE ELSE,
AS A MYSTERY OF LIGHT. GAZING UPON MARY, WE COME TO KNOW
THE TRANSFORMING POWER PRESENT IN THE EUCHARIST.
IN HER WE SEE THE WORLD RENEWED IN LOVE.
CONTEMPLATING HER, ASSUMED BODY AND SOUL INTO HEAVEN,
WE SEE OPENING UP BEFORE US THOSE "NEW HEAVENS" AND
THAT "NEW EARTH" WHICH WILL APPEAR AT THE SECOND COMING
OF CHRIST. HERE BELOW, THE EUCHARIST REPRESENTS
THEIR PLEDGE, AND IN A CERTAIN WAY, THEIR ANTICIPATION:
"VENI, DOMINE IESU!" (*REV* 22:20).

Ecclesia de Eucharistia (62)

Mother Teresa receives Holy Communion from the Holy Father in the Philippines, 1981.

FATHER I AM HUNGRY … GIVE THIS SOUL HER FOOD, HER LORD IN THE EUCHARIST.

St. Catherine of Siena

THE CULMINATION OF THE MASS IS NOT THE CONSECRATION, BUT COMMUNION.

St. Maximilian Kolbe

Top: The Pope venerates the tomb of St. Catherine of Siena, Rome, 1978. Bottom: James Currey, O.F.M., Conv. presents a portrait of St. Maximilian Kolbe to the Pope. Currey once told the Holy Father, "I want you to dedicate the world to Maximilian Kolbe;" to which the Pope swiftly replied, "You do that." Opposite: The crowd that gathered in St. Peter's Square for Padre Pio's canonization spills into the streets of Rome, 2002.

WHEN YOU LOOK AT THE CRUCIFIX, YOU UNDERSTAND
HOW MUCH JESUS LOVED YOU THEN. WHEN YOU LOOK AT THE SACRED HOST YOU
UNDERSTAND HOW MUCH JESUS LOVES YOU NOW.

Mother Teresa of Calcutta

Top left: The Holy Father prays before an image of Christ as Divine Mercy in Poland, 1997. Top right: Maximilian Kolbe's canonization Mass in October, 1982. Bottom: The Pope venerates a relic in Poland, 1997.

Bone pastor, panis vere,

Iesu, nostri, miserere ...

Come then, good Shepherd, bread divine,

Still show to us thy mercy sign;

Oh, feed us, still keep us thine;

So we may see thy glories shine in fields of immortality.

O thou, the wisest, mightiest, best,

Our present food, our future rest,

Come, make us each thy chosen guest,

Co-heirs of thine, and comrades blest

With saints whose dwelling is with thee.

St. Thomas Aquinas

MAY HE, WHO INVITES YOU TO THE ONE TABLE AND
FEEDS YOU WITH THE ONE BREAD, MAKE YOU ONE IN HEART AND MIND. AMEN.

Blessing and Dismissal, Rite of Dedication of an Altar

Remain in peace, O holy altar of God,

I hope to return to you in peace.

May the offering I have received from you

forgive my sins and prepare me to stand blameless

before the throne of Christ.

I know not whether I will be able to return

to you again to offer sacrifice.

Guard me, O Lord,

and protect your holy Church,

that she may be the way to salvation and

the light of the world.

Amen.

Maronite Liturgy

ENCYCLICAL LETTER

Ecclesia de Eucharistia

OF HIS HOLINESS POPE JOHN PAUL II

TO THE BISHOPS PRIESTS AND DEACONS

MEN AND WOMEN

IN THE CONSECRATED LIFE AND ALL THE LAY FAITHFUL

ON THE EUCHARIST IN ITS RELATIONSHIP TO THE CHURCH

INTRODUCTION

1. The Church draws her life from the Eucharist. This truth does not simply express a daily experience of faith, but recapitulates *the heart of the mystery of the Church.* In a variety of ways, she joyfully experiences the constant fulfillment of the promise: "Lo, I am with you always, to the close of the age" (*Mt* 28:20), but in the Holy Eucharist, through the changing of bread and wine into the body and blood of the Lord, she rejoices in this presence with unique intensity. Ever since Pentecost, when the Church, the People of the New Covenant, began her pilgrim journey toward her heavenly homeland, the Divine Sacrament has continued to mark the passing of her days, filling them with confident hope.

The Second Vatican Council rightly proclaimed that the eucharistic sacrifice is "the source and summit of the Christian life."[1] "For the most holy Eucharist contains the Church's entire spiritual wealth: Christ himself, our Passover and living bread. Through his own flesh, now made living and life-giving by the Holy Spirit, he offers life to men."[2] Consequently, the gaze of the Church is constantly turned to her Lord, present in the Sacrament of the Altar, in which she discovers the full manifestation of his boundless love.

2. During the Great Jubilee of the Year 2000, I had an opportunity to celebrate the Eucharist in the Cenacle of Jerusalem where, according to tradition,-. *The Upper Room was where this most holy Sacrament was instituted.* It is there that Christ took bread, broke it and gave it to his disciples, saying: "Take this, all of you, and eat it: this is my body which will be given up for you" (cf. *Mt* 26:26; *Lk* 22:19; *1 Cor* 11:24). Then he took the cup of wine and said to them: "Take this, all of you and drink from it: this is the cup of my blood, the blood of the new and everlasting covenant. It will be shed for you and for all, so that sins may be forgiven" (cf. *Mk* 14:24; *Lk* 22:20; *1 Cor* 11:25). I am grateful to the Lord Jesus for allowing me to repeat in that same place, in obedience to his command: "Do this in memory of me" (*Lk* 22:19), the words which he spoke two-thousand years ago.

Did the Apostles who took part in the Last Supper understand the meaning of the words spoken by Christ? Perhaps not. Those words would only be fully clear at the end of the *Triduum sacrum*, the time from Thursday evening to Sunday morning. Those days embrace the *mysterium paschale*; they also embrace the *mysterium eucharisticum*.

3. The Church was born of the paschal mystery. For this very reason the Eucharist, which is in an outstanding way the sacrament of the paschal mystery, *stands at the center of the Church's life.* This is already clear from the earliest images of the Church found in the Acts of the Apostles: "They devoted themselves to the Apostles' teaching and fellowship, to the breaking of bread and the prayers" (2:42). The "breaking of the bread" refers to the Eucharist. Two-thousand years later, we continue to relive that primordial image of the Church. At every celebration of the Eucharist, we are spiritually brought back to the paschal Triduum: to the events of the evening of Holy Thursday, to the Last Supper and to what followed it. The institution of the Eucharist sacramentally anticipated the events which were about to take place, beginning with the agony in Gethsemane. Once again we see Jesus as he leaves the Upper Room, descends with his disciples to the Kidron valley and goes to the Garden of Olives. Even today that Garden shelters some very ancient olive trees. Perhaps they witnessed what happened beneath their shade that evening, when Christ in prayer was filled with anguish "and his sweat became like drops of blood falling down upon the ground" (*Lk* 22:44). The blood which shortly before he had given to the Church as the drink of salvation in the sacrament of the Eucharist, *began to be shed*; its outpouring would then be completed on Golgotha to become the means of our redemption: "Christ ... as high priest of the good things to come ..., entered once and for all into the Holy Place, taking not the blood of goats and calves but his own blood, thus securing an eternal redemption" (*Heb* 9:11-12).

4. *The hour of our redemption*. Although deeply troubled, Jesus does not flee before his "hour." "And what shall I say? 'Father, save me from this hour?' No, for this purpose I have come to this hour" (*Jn* 12:27). He wanted his disciples to keep him company, yet he had to experience loneliness and abandonment: "So, could you not watch with me one hour? Watch and pray that you may not enter into temptation" (*Mt* 26:40-41). Only John would remain at the foot of the cross, at the side of Mary and the faithful women. The agony in Gethsemane was the introduction to the agony of the cross on Good Friday. *The holy hour*, the hour of the redemption of the world. Whenever the Eucharist is celebrated at the tomb of Jesus in Jerusalem, there is an almost tangible return to his "hour," the hour of his cross and glorification. Every priest who celebrates Holy Mass, together with the Christian community which takes part in it, is led back in spirit to that place and that hour.

"He was crucified, he suffered death and was buried; he descended to the dead; on the third day he rose again." The words of the profession of faith are echoed by the words of contemplation and proclamation: *"This is the wood of the cross, on which hung the Savior of the world. Come, let us worship."* This is the invitation which the Church extends to all in the afternoon hours of Good Friday. She then takes up her song during the Easter season in order to proclaim: *"The Lord is risen from the tomb; for our sake he hung on the cross, Alleluia."*

5. *"Mysterium fidei!*-The Mystery of Faith!" When the priest recites or chants these words, all present acclaim: "We announce your death, O Lord, and we proclaim your resurrection, until you come in glory."

In these or similar words, the Church, while pointing to Christ in the mystery of his passion, *also reveals her own mystery: Ecclesia de Eucharistia*. By the gift of the Holy Spirit at Pentecost the Church was born and set out upon the pathways of the world, yet a decisive moment in her taking shape was certainly the institution of the Eucharist in the Upper Room. Her foundation and wellspring is the whole *Triduum paschale*, but this is as it were gathered up, foreshadowed and "concentrated" for ever in the gift of the Eucharist. In this gift Jesus Christ entrusted to his Church the perennial making present of the paschal mystery. With it he brought about a mysterious "oneness in time" between that *Triduum* and the passage of the centuries.

The thought of this leads us to profound amazement and gratitude. In the paschal event and the Eucharist which makes it present throughout the centuries, there is a truly enormous "capacity" which embraces all of history as the recipient of the grace of the redemption. This amazement should always fill the Church assembled for the celebration of the Eucharist. But in a special way it should fill the minister of the Eucharist. For it is he who, by the authority given him in the sacrament of priestly ordination, effects the consecration. It is he who says with the power coming to him from Christ in the Upper Room: "This is my body which will be given up for you. This is the cup of my blood, poured out for you ..." The priest says these words, or rather *he puts his voice at the disposal of the One who spoke these words in the Upper Room* and who desires that they should be repeated in every generation by all those who in the Church ministerially share in his priesthood.

6. I would like to rekindle this eucharistic "amazement" by the present encyclical letter, in continuity with the Jubilee heritage which I have left to the Church in the apostolic letter *Novo Millennio Ineunte* and its Marian crowning *Rosarium Virginis Mariae*. To contemplate the face of Christ, and to contemplate it with Mary, is the "program" which I have set before the Church at the dawn of the third millennium, summoning her to put out into the deep on the sea of history with the enthusiasm of the new evangelization. To contemplate Christ involves being able to recognize him wherever he manifests himself, in his many forms of presence, but above all in the living sacrament of his body and his blood. *The Church draws her life from Christ in the Eucharist*; by him she is fed and by him she is enlightened. The Eucharist is both a mystery of faith and a "mystery of light."[3] Whenever the Church celebrates the Eucharist, the faithful can in some way relive the experience of the two disciples on the road to Emmaus: "their eyes were opened and they recognized him" (*Lk* 24:31).

7. From the time I began my ministry as the Successor of Peter, I have always marked Holy Thursday, the day of the Eucharist and of the priesthood, by sending a letter to all the priests of the world. This year, the twenty-fifth of my pontificate, I wish to involve the whole Church more fully in this eucharistic reflection, also as a way of thanking the Lord for the gift of the Eucharist and the priesthood: "Gift and Mystery."[4] By proclaiming the Year of the Rosary, I wish to put this, my twenty-fifth anniversary, *under the aegis of the contemplation of Christ at the school of Mary*. Consequently, I cannot let this Holy Thursday 2003 pass without halting before the "eucharistic face" of Christ and pointing out with new force to the Church the centrality of the Eucharist.

From it the Church draws her life. From this "living bread" she draws her nourishment. How could I not feel the need to urge everyone to experience it ever anew?

8. When I think of the Eucharist, and look at my life as a priest, as a bishop and as the Successor of Peter, I naturally recall the many times and places in which I was able to celebrate it. I remember the parish church of Niegowić, where I had my first pastoral assignment, the collegiate church of Saint Florian in Krakow, Wawel Cathedral, Saint Peter's Basilica and so many basilicas and churches in Rome and throughout the world. I have been able to celebrate Holy Mass in chapels built along mountain paths, on lakeshores and seacoasts; I have celebrated it on altars built in stadiums and in city squares ... This varied scenario of celebrations of the Eucharist has given me a powerful experience of its universal and, so to speak, cosmic character. Yes, cosmic! Because even when it is celebrated on the humble altar of a country church, the Eucharist is always in some way celebrated *on the altar of the world*. It unites heaven and earth. It embraces and permeates all creation. The Son of God became man in order to restore all creation, in one supreme act of praise, to the One who made it from nothing. He, the Eternal High Priest who by the blood of his cross entered the eternal sanctuary, thus gives back

to the Creator and Father all creation redeemed. He does so through the priestly ministry of the Church, to the glory of the Most Holy Trinity. Truly this is the *mysterium fidei* which is accomplished in the Eucharist: the world which came forth from the hands of God the Creator now returns to him redeemed by Christ.

9. The Eucharist, as Christ's saving presence in the community of the faithful and its spiritual food, is the most precious possession which the Church can have in her journey through history. This explains the *lively concern* which she has always shown for the eucharistic mystery, a concern which finds authoritative expression in the work of the Councils and the Popes. How can we not admire the doctrinal expositions of the Decrees on the Most Holy Eucharist and on the Holy Sacrifice of the Mass promulgated by the Council of Trent? For centuries those Decrees guided theology and catechesis, and they are still a dogmatic reference point for the continual renewal and growth of God's People in faith and in love for the Eucharist. In times closer to our own, three encyclical letters should be mentioned: the Encyclical *Mirae Caritatis* of Leo XIII (28 May 1902),[5] the encyclical *Mediator Dei* of Pius XII (20 November 1947)[6] and the Encyclical *Mysterium Fidei* of Paul VI (3 September 1965)[7]

The Second Vatican Council, while not issuing a specific document on the eucharistic mystery, considered its various aspects throughout its documents, especially the Dogmatic Constitution on the Church, *Lumen Gentium* and the Constitution on the Sacred Liturgy, *Sacrosanctum Concilium*.

I myself, in the first years of my apostolic ministry in the Chair of Peter, wrote the apostolic letter *Dominicae Cenae* (24 February 1980),[8] in which I discussed some aspects of the eucharistic mystery and its importance for the life of those who are its ministers. Today I take up anew the thread of that argument, with even greater emotion and gratitude in my heart, echoing as it were the word of the Psalmist: "What shall I render to the Lord for all his bounty to me? I will lift up the cup of salvation and call on the name of the Lord" (Ps 116:12-13).

10. The Magisterium's commitment to proclaiming the eucharistic mystery has been matched by interior growth within the Christian community. Certainly *the liturgical reform inaugurated by the Council* has greatly contributed to a more conscious, active and fruitful participation in the Holy Sacrifice of the Altar on the part of the faithful. In many places, *adoration of the Blessed Sacrament* is also an important daily practice and becomes an inexhaustible source of holiness. The devout participation of the faithful in the eucharistic procession on the Solemnity of the Body and Blood of Christ is a grace from the Lord which yearly brings joy to those who take part in it.

Other positive signs of eucharistic faith and love might also be mentioned. Unfortunately, alongside these lights, *there are also shadows*. In some places the practice of eucharistic adoration has been almost completely abandoned. In various parts of the Church, abuses have occurred, leading to confusion with regard to sound faith and Catholic doctrine concerning this wonderful sacrament. At times one encounters an extremely reductive understanding of the eucharistic mystery. Stripped of its sacrificial meaning, it is celebrated as if it were simply a fraternal banquet. Furthermore, the necessity of the ministerial priesthood, grounded in apostolic succession, is at times obscured and the sacramental nature of the Eucharist is reduced to its mere effectiveness as a form of proclamation. This has led here and there to ecumenical initiatives which, albeit well-intentioned, indulge in eucharistic practices contrary to the discipline by which the Church expresses her faith. How can we not express profound grief at all this? The Eucharist is too great a gift to tolerate ambiguity and depreciation.

It is my hope that the present encyclical letter will effectively help to banish the dark clouds of unacceptable doctrine and practice, so that the Eucharist will continue to shine forth in all its radiant mystery.

CHAPTER ONE
THE MYSTERY OF FAITH

11. "The Lord Jesus on the night he was betrayed" (*1 Cor* 11:23) instituted the eucharistic sacrifice of his body and his blood. The words of the Apostle Paul bring us back to the dramatic setting in which the Eucharist was born. The Eucharist is indelibly marked by the event of the Lord's passion and death, of which it is not only a reminder but the sacramental re-presentation. It is the sacrifice of the cross perpetuated down the ages.[9] This truth is well expressed by the words with which the assembly in the Latin rite responds to the priest's proclamation of the "Mystery of Faith": *"We announce your death, O Lord."*

The Church has received the Eucharist from Christ her Lord not as one gift-however precious-among so many others, but as the *gift par excellence*, for it is the gift of himself, of his person in his sacred humanity, as well as the gift of his saving work. Nor does it remain confined to the past, since "all that Christ is-all that he did and suffered for all men-participates in the divine eternity, and so transcends all times."[10]

When the Church celebrates the Eucharist, the memorial of her Lord's death and resurrection, this central event of salvation becomes really present and "the work of our redemption is carried out."[11] This sacrifice is so decisive for the salvation of the human race that Jesus Christ offered it and returned to the Father only *after he had left us a means of sharing in it* as if we had been present there. Each member of the faithful can thus take part in it and inexhaustibly gain its fruits. This is the faith from which generations of Christians down the ages have lived. The Church's Magisterium has constantly reaffirmed this faith with joyful gratitude for its inestimable gift.[12] I wish once more to recall this truth and to join you, my dear brothers and sisters, in adoration before this mystery: a great mystery, a mystery of mercy. What more could Jesus have done for us? Truly, in the Eucharist, he shows us a love which goes "to the end" (cf. *Jn* 13:1), a love which knows no measure.

12. This aspect of the universal charity of the eucharistic sacrifice is based on the words of the Savior himself. In instituting it, he did not merely say: "This is my body," "this is my blood," but went on to add: "which is given for you," "which is poured out for you" (*Lk* 22:19-20). Jesus did not simply state that what he was giving them to eat and drink was his body and his blood; he also expressed *its sacrificial meaning* and made sacramentally present his sacrifice which would soon be offered on the cross for the salvation of all. "The Mass is at the same time, and inseparably, the sacrificial memorial in which the sacrifice of the cross is perpetuated and the sacred banquet of communion with the Lord's body and blood."[13]

The Church constantly draws her life from the redeeming sacrifice; she approaches it not only through faith-filled remembrance, but also through a real contact, since *this sacrifice is made present ever anew*, sacramentally perpetuated, in every community which offers it at the hands of the consecrated minister. The Eucharist thus applies to men and women today the reconciliation won once and for all by Christ for mankind in every age. "The sacrifice of Christ and the sacrifice of the Eucharist are *one single sacrifice.*"[14] Saint John Chrysostom put it well: "We always offer the same Lamb, not one today and another tomorrow, but always the same one. For this reason the sacrifice is always only one ... Even now we offer that victim who was once offered and who will never be consumed."[15]

The Mass makes present the sacrifice of the cross; it does not add to that sacrifice nor does it multiply it.[16] What is repeated is its *memorial* celebration, its "commemorative representation" (*memorialis demonstratio*),[17] which makes Christ's one, definitive redemptive sacrifice always present in time. The sacrificial nature of the eucharistic mystery cannot therefore be understood as something separate, independent of the cross or only indirectly referring to the sacrifice of Calvary.

13. By virtue of its close relationship to the sacrifice of Golgotha, the Eucharist is *a sacrifice in the strict sense*, and not only in a general way, as if it were simply a matter of Christ's offering himself to the faithful as their spiritual food. The gift of his love and obedience to the point of giving his life (cf. *Jn* 10:17-18) is in the first place a gift to his Father. Certainly it is a gift given for our sake, and indeed that of all humanity (cf. *Mt* 26:28; *Mk* 14:24; *Lk* 22:20; *Jn* 10:15), yet it is *first and foremost a gift to the Father*: "a sacrifice that the Father accepted, giving, in return for this total self-giving by his Son, who 'became obedient unto death' (*Phil* 2:8), his own paternal gift, that is to say the grant of new immortal life in the resurrection."[18]

In giving his sacrifice to the Church, Christ has also made his own the spiritual sacrifice of the Church, which is called to offer herself in union with the sacrifice of Christ. This is the teaching of the Second Vatican Council concerning all the faithful: "Taking part in the eucharistic sacrifice, which is the source and summit of the whole Christian life, they offer the divine victim to God, and offer themselves along with it."[19]

14. Christ's Passover includes not only his passion and death, but also his resurrection. This is recalled by the assembly's acclamation following the consecration: *"We proclaim your resurrection."* The eucharistic sacrifice makes present not only the mystery of the Savior's passion and death, but also the mystery of the resurrection which crowned his sacrifice. It is as the living and risen One that Christ can become, in the Eucharist, the "bread of life" (*Jn* 6:35, 48), the "living bread" (*Jn* 6:51). Saint Ambrose reminded the newly-initiated that the Eucharist applies the event of the resurrection to their lives: "Today Christ is yours, yet each day he rises again for you."[20] Saint Cyril of Alexandria also makes clear that sharing in the sacred mysteries "is a true confession and a remembrance that the Lord died and returned to life for us and on our behalf."[21]

15. The sacramental re-presentation of Christ's sacrifice, crowned by the resurrection, in the Mass involves a most special presence which—in the words of Paul VI—"is called 'real' not as a way of excluding all other types of presence as if they were 'not real,' but because it is a presence in the fullest sense: a substantial presence whereby Christ, the God-Man, is wholly and entirely present."[22] This sets forth once more the perennially valid teaching of the Council of Trent: "the consecration of the bread and wine effects the change of the whole substance of the bread into the substance of the body of Christ our Lord, and of the whole substance of the wine into the substance of his blood. And the holy Catholic Church has fittingly and properly called this change transubstantiation."[23] Truly the Eucharist is a *mysterium fidei*, a mystery which surpasses our understanding and can only be received in faith, as is often brought out in the catechesis of the Church Fathers regarding this divine sacrament: "Do not see—Saint Cyril of Jerusalem exhorts—in the bread and wine merely natural elements, because the Lord has expressly said that they are his body and his blood: faith assures you of this, though your senses suggest otherwise."[24]

Adoro te devote, latens Deitas, we shall continue to sing with the Angelic Doctor. Before this mystery of love, human reason fully experiences its limitations. One understands how, down the centuries, this truth has stimulated theology to strive to understand it ever more deeply.

These are praiseworthy efforts, which are all the more helpful and insightful to the extent that they are able to join critical thinking to the "living faith" of the Church, as grasped especially by the Magisterium's "sure charism of truth" and the "intimate sense of spiritual realities"[25] which is attained above all by the saints. There remains the boundary indicated by Paul VI: "Every theological explanation which seeks some understanding of this mystery, in order to be in accord with Catholic faith, must firmly maintain that in objective reality, independently of our mind, the bread and wine have ceased to exist after the consecration, so that the adorable body and blood of the Lord Jesus from that moment on are really before us under the sacramental species of bread and wine."[26]

16. The saving efficacy of the sacrifice is fully realized when the Lord's body and blood are received in Communion. The eucharistic sacrifice is intrinsically directed to the inward union of the faithful with Christ through Communion; we receive the very One who offered himself for us, we receive his body which he gave up for us on the cross and his blood which he "poured out for many for the forgiveness of sins" (*Mt* 26:28). We are reminded of his words: "As the living Father sent me, and I live because of the Father, so he who eats me will live because of me" (*Jn* 6:57). Jesus himself reassures us that this union, which he compares to that of the life of the Trinity, is truly realized. *The Eucharist is a true banquet,* in which Christ offers himself as our nourishment. When for the first time Jesus spoke of this food, his listeners were astonished and bewildered, which forced the Master to emphasize the objective truth of his words: "Truly, truly, I say to you, unless you eat the flesh of the Son of Man and drink his blood, you have no life within you" (*Jn* 6:53). This is no metaphorical food: "My flesh is food indeed, and my blood is drink indeed" (*Jn* 6:55).

17. Through our communion in his body and blood, Christ also grants us his Spirit. Saint Ephrem writes: "He called the bread his living body and he filled it with himself and his Spirit … He who eats it with faith, eats Fire and Spirit … Take and eat this, all of you, and eat with it the Holy Spirit. For it is truly my body and whoever eats it will have eternal life."[27] The Church implores this divine gift, the source of every other gift, in the eucharistic epiclesis. In the *Divine Liturgy* of Saint John Chrysostom, for example, we find the prayer: "We beseech, implore and beg you: send your Holy Spirit upon us all and upon these gifts … that those who partake of them may be purified in soul, receive the forgiveness of their sins, and share in the Holy Spirit."[28] And in the Roman Missal the celebrant prays: "grant that we who are nourished by his body and blood may be filled with his Holy Spirit, and become one body, one spirit in Christ."[29] Thus by the gift of his body and blood Christ increases within us the gift of his Spirit, already poured out in baptism and bestowed as a "seal" in the sacrament of Confirmation.

18. The acclamation of the assembly following the consecration appropriately ends by expressing the eschatological thrust which marks the celebration of the Eucharist (cf. *1 Cor* 11:26): *"until you come in glory."* The Eucharist is a straining toward the goal, a foretaste of the fullness of joy promised by Christ (cf. *Jn* 15:11); it is in some way the anticipation of heaven, the "pledge of future glory."[30] In the Eucharist, everything speaks of confident waiting "in joyful hope for the coming of our Savior, Jesus Christ."[31] Those who feed on Christ in the Eucharist need not wait until the hereafter to receive eternal life: *they already possess it on earth*, as the first-fruits of a future fullness which will embrace man in his totality. For in the Eucharist we also receive the pledge of our bodily resurrection at the end of the world: "He who eats my flesh and drinks my blood has eternal life, and I will raise him up at the last day" (*Jn* 6:54). This pledge of the future resurrection comes from the fact that the flesh of the Son of Man, given as food, is his body in its glorious state after the resurrection. With the Eucharist we digest, as it were, the "secret" of the resurrection. For this reason Saint Ignatius of Antioch rightly defined the eucharistic Bread as "a medicine of immortality, an antidote to death."[32]

19. The eschatological tension kindled by the Eucharist *expresses and reinforces our communion with the Church in heaven.* It is not by chance that the Eastern Anaphoras and the Latin Eucharistic Prayers honor Mary, the ever-Virgin Mother of Jesus Christ our Lord and God, the angels, the holy apostles, the glorious martyrs and all the saints. This is an aspect of the Eucharist which merits greater attention: in celebrating the sacrifice of the Lamb, we are united to the heavenly "liturgy" and become part of that great multitude which cries out: "Salvation belongs to our God who sits upon the throne, and to the Lamb!" (*Rev* 7:10). The Eucharist is truly a glimpse of heaven appearing on earth. It is a glorious ray of the heavenly Jerusalem which pierces the clouds of our history and lights up our journey.

20. A significant consequence of the eschatological tension inherent in the Eucharist is also the fact that it spurs us on our journey through history and plants a seed of living hope in our daily commitment to the work before us. Certainly the Christian vision leads to the expectation of "new heavens" and "a new earth" (*Rev* 21:1), but this increases, rather than lessens, *our sense of responsibility for the world today.*[33] I wish to reaffirm this forcefully at the beginning of the new millennium, so that Christians will feel more obliged than ever not to neglect their duties as citizens in this world. Theirs is the task of contributing with the light of the gospel to the building of a more human world, a world fully in harmony with God's plan.

Many problems darken the horizon of our time. We need but think of the urgent need to work for peace, to base relationships between peoples on solid premises of justice and solidarity, and to defend human life from conception to its natural end. And what should we say of the thousand inconsistencies of a "globalized" world where the weakest, the most powerless and the poorest appear to have so little hope! It is in this world that Christian hope must shine forth! For this reason too, the Lord wished to remain with us in the Eucharist, making his presence in meal and sacrifice the promise of a humanity renewed by his love. Significantly, in their account of the Last Supper, the Synoptics recount the institution of the Eucharist, while the Gospel of John relates, as a way of bringing out its profound meaning, the account of the "washing of the feet," in which Jesus appears as the teacher of communion and of service (cf. *Jn* 13:1-20). The Apostle Paul, for his part, says that it is "unworthy" of a Christian community to partake of the Lord's Supper amid division and indifference toward the poor (cf. *1 Cor* 11:17-22, 27-34).[34]

Proclaiming the death of the Lord "until he comes" (*1 Cor* 11:26) entails that all who take part in the Eucharist be committed to changing their lives and making them in a certain way completely "eucharistic." It is this fruit of a transfigured existence and a commitment to transforming the world in accordance with the gospel which splendidly illustrates the eschatological tension inherent in the celebration of the Eucharist and in the Christian life as a whole: "Come, Lord Jesus!" (*Rev* 22:20).

CHAPTER TWO
THE EUCHARIST BUILDS THE CHURCH

21. The Second Vatican Council teaches that the celebration of the Eucharist is at the center of the process of the Church's growth. After stating that "the Church, as the Kingdom of Christ already present in mystery, grows visibly in the world through the power of God,"[35] then, as if in answer to the question: "How does the Church grow?" the Council adds: "as often as the sacrifice of the cross by which 'Christ our Pasch is sacrificed' (*1 Cor* 5:7) is celebrated on the altar, the work of our redemption is carried out. At the same time in the sacrament of the eucharistic bread, the unity of the faithful, who form one body in Christ (cf. *1 Cor* 10:17), is both expressed and brought about."[36]

A causal influence of the Eucharist is present at the Church's very origins. The Evangelists specify that it was the Twelve, the Apostles, who gathered with Jesus at the Last Supper (cf. *Mt* 26:20; *Mk* 14:17; *Lk* 22:14). This is a detail of notable importance, for the Apostles "were both the seeds of the new Israel and the beginning of the sacred hierarchy."[37] By offering them his body and his blood as food, Christ mysteriously involved them in the sacrifice which would be completed later on Calvary. By analogy with the Covenant of Mount Sinai, sealed by sacrifice and the sprinkling of blood,[38] the actions and words of Jesus at the Last Supper laid the foundations of the new messianic community, the People of the New Covenant.

The Apostles, by accepting in the Upper Room Jesus' invitation: "Take, eat," "Drink of it, all of you" (*Mt* 26:26-27), entered for the first time into Sacramental Communion with him. From that time forward, until the end of the age, the Church is built up through Sacramental Communion with the Son of God who was sacrificed for our sake: "Do this is remembrance of me. … Do this, as often as you drink it, in remembrance of me" (*1 Cor* 11:24-25; cf. *Lk* 22:19).

22. Incorporation into Christ, which is brought about by baptism, is constantly renewed and consolidated by sharing in the eucharistic sacrifice, especially by that full sharing which takes place in Sacramental Communion. We can say not only that *each of us receives Christ*, but also that *Christ receives each of us*. He enters into friendship with us: "You are my friends" (*Jn* 15:14). Indeed, it is because of him that we have life: "He who eats me will live because of me" (*Jn* 6:57). Eucharistic Communion brings about in a sublime way the mutual "abiding" of Christ and each of his followers: "Abide in me, and I in you" (*Jn* 15:4).

By its union with Christ, the People of the New Covenant, far from closing in upon itself, becomes a "sacrament" for humanity,[39] a sign and instrument of the salvation achieved by Christ, the light of the world and the salt of the earth (cf. *Mt* 5:13-16), for the redemption of all.[40] The Church's mission stands in continuity with the mission of Christ: "As the Father has sent me, even so I send you" (*Jn* 20:21). From the perpetuation of the sacrifice of the cross and her communion with the body and blood of Christ in the Eucharist, the Church draws the spiritual power needed to carry out her mission. The Eucharist thus appears as both *the source* and *the summit* of all evangelization, since its goal is the communion of mankind with Christ and, in him, with the Father and the Holy Spirit.[41]

23. Eucharistic Communion also confirms the Church in her unity as the body of Christ. Saint Paul refers to this *unifying power* of participation in the banquet of the Eucharist when he writes to the Corinthians: "The bread which we break, is it not a communion in the body of Christ? Because there is one bread, we who are many are one body, for we all partake of the one bread" (*1 Cor* 10:16-17). Saint John Chrysostom's commentary on these words is profound and perceptive: "For what is the bread? It is the body of Christ. And what do those who receive it become? The body of Christ—not many bodies but one body. For as bread is completely one, though made of up many grains of wheat, and these, albeit unseen, remain nonetheless present, in such a way that their difference is not apparent since they have been made a perfect whole, so too are we mutually joined to one another and together united with Christ."[42] The argument is compelling: our union with Christ, which is a gift and grace for each of us, makes it possible for us, in him, to share in the unity of his body which is the Church. The Eucharist reinforces the incorporation into Christ which took place in baptism though the gift of the Spirit (cf. *1 Cor* 12:13, 27).

The joint and inseparable activity of the Son and of the Holy Spirit, which is at the origin of the Church, of her consolidation and her continued life, is at work in the Eucharist. This was clearly evident to the author of the *Liturgy of Saint James:* in the epiclesis of the Anaphora, God the Father is asked to send the Holy Spirit upon the faithful and upon the offerings, so that the body and blood of Christ "may be a help to all those who partake of it … for the sanctification of their souls and bodies."[43] The Church is fortified by the divine Paraclete through the sanctification of the faithful in the Eucharist.

24. The gift of Christ and his Spirit which we receive in eucharistic Communion superabundantly fulfills the yearning for fraternal unity deeply rooted in the human heart; at the same time, it elevates the experience of fraternity already present in our common sharing at the same eucharistic table to a degree which far surpasses that of the simple human experience of sharing a meal. Through her communion with the body of Christ, the Church comes to be ever more profoundly "in Christ in the nature of a sacrament, that is, a sign and instrument of intimate unity with God and of the unity of the whole human race."[44]

The seeds of disunity, which daily experience shows to be so deeply rooted in humanity as a result of sin, are countered by *the unifying power* of the body of Christ. The Eucharist, precisely by building up the Church, creates human community.

25. The *worship of the Eucharist outside of the Mass* is of inestimable value for the life of the Church. This worship is strictly linked to the celebration of the eucharistic sacrifice. The presence of Christ under the sacred species reserved after Mass-a presence which lasts as long as

the species of bread and of wine remain [45]—derives from the celebration of the sacrifice and is directed toward communion, both sacramental and spiritual.[46] It is the responsibility of pastors to encourage, also by their personal witness, the practice of eucharistic adoration, and exposition of the Blessed Sacrament in particular, as well as prayer of adoration before Christ present under the eucharistic species.[47]

It is pleasant to spend time with him, to lie close to his breast like the Beloved Disciple (cf. *Jn* 13:25) and to feel the infinite love present in his heart. If in our time Christians must be distinguished above all by the "art of prayer,"[48] how can we not feel a renewed need to spend time in spiritual converse, in silent adoration, in heartfelt love before Christ present in the Most Holy Sacrament? How often, dear brother and sisters, have I experienced this, and drawn from it strength, consolation and support!

This practice, repeatedly praised and recommended by the Magisterium,[49] is supported by the example of many saints. Particularly outstanding in this regard was Saint Alphonsus Liguori, who wrote: "Of all devotions, that of adoring Jesus in the Blessed Sacrament is the greatest after the sacraments, the one dearest to God and the one most helpful to us."[50] The Eucharist is a priceless treasure: by not only celebrating it but also by praying before it outside of Mass we are enabled to make contact with the very wellspring of grace. A Christian community desirous of contemplating the face of Christ in the spirit which I proposed in the apostolic letters *Novo Millennio Ineunte* and *Rosarium Virginis Mariae* cannot fail also to develop this aspect of eucharistic worship, which prolongs and increases the fruits of our communion in the body and blood of the Lord.

CHAPTER THREE
THE APOSTOLICITY OF THE EUCHARIST AND OF THE CHURCH

26. If, as I have said, the Eucharist builds the Church and the Church makes the Eucharist, it follows that there is a profound relationship between the two, so much so that we can apply to the eucharistic mystery the very words with which, in the Nicene-Constantinopolitan Creed, we profess the Church to be "one, holy, catholic and apostolic." The Eucharist too is one and catholic. It is also holy, indeed, the Most Holy Sacrament. But it is above all its apostolicity that we must now consider.

27. The *Catechism of the Catholic Church*, in explaining how the Church is apostolic-founded on the Apostles-sees *three meanings* in this expression. First, "she was and remains built on 'the foundation of the Apostles' (*Eph* 2:20), the witnesses chosen and sent on mission by Christ himself."[51] The Eucharist too has its foundation in the Apostles, not in the sense that it did not originate in Christ himself, but because it was entrusted by Jesus to the Apostles and has been handed down to us by them and by their successors. It is in continuity with the practice of the Apostles, in obedience to the Lord's command, that the Church has celebrated the Eucharist down the centuries.

The second sense in which the Church is apostolic, as the *Catechism* points out, is that "with the help of the Spirit dwelling in her, the Church keeps and hands on the teaching, the 'good deposit,' the salutary words she has heard from the Apostles."[52] Here too the Eucharist is apostolic, for it is celebrated in conformity with the faith of the Apostles. At various times in the two-thousand-year history of the People of the New Covenant, the Church's Magisterium has more precisely defined her teaching on the Eucharist, including its proper terminology, precisely in order to safeguard the apostolic faith with regard to this sublime mystery. This faith remains unchanged and it is essential for the Church that it remain unchanged.

28. Lastly, the Church is apostolic in the sense that she "continues to be taught, sanctified and guided by the Apostles until Christ's return, through their successors in pastoral office: the college of Bishops assisted by priests, in union with the Successor of Peter, the Church's supreme pastor."[53] Succession to the Apostles in the pastoral mission necessarily entails the sacrament of Holy Orders, that is, the uninterrupted sequence, from the very beginning, of valid episcopal ordinations.[54] This succession is essential for the Church to exist in a proper and full sense.

The Eucharist also expresses this sense of apostolicity. As the Second Vatican Council teaches, "the faithful join in the offering of the Eucharist by virtue of their royal priesthood,"[55] yet it is the ordained priest who, "acting in the person of Christ, brings about the eucharistic sacrifice and offers it to God in the name of all the people."[56] For this reason, the Roman Missal prescribes that only the priest should recite the eucharistic prayer, while the people participate in faith and in silence.[57]

29. The expression repeatedly employed by the Second Vatican Council, according to which "the ministerial priest, acting in the person of Christ, brings about the eucharistic sacrifice,"[58] was already firmly rooted in papal teaching.[59] As I have pointed out on other occasions, the phrase *in persona Christi* "means more than offering 'in the name of' or 'in the place of' Christ. In persona means in specific sacramental identification with the eternal High Priest who is the author and principal subject of this sacrifice of his, a sacrifice in which, in truth, nobody can take his place."[60] The ministry of priests who have received the sacrament of Holy Orders, in the economy of salvation chosen by Christ, makes clear that the Eucharist which they celebrate is *a gift which radically transcends the power of the assembly* and is in any event essential for validly linking the eucharistic consecration to the sacrifice of the cross and to the Last Supper. The assembly gathered together for the celebration of the Eucharist, if it is to be a truly eucharistic assembly, absolutely requires the presence of an ordained priest as its president. On the other hand, the community is by itself incapable of providing an ordained minister. This minister is a gift which the assembly *receives through episcopal succession going back to the Apostles*. It is the Bishop who, through the Sacrament of Holy Orders, makes a new presbyter by conferring upon him the power to consecrate the Eucharist. Consequently, "the eucharistic mystery cannot be celebrated in any community except by an ordained priest, as the Fourth Lateran Council expressly taught."[61]

30. The Catholic Church's teaching on the relationship between priestly ministry and the Eucharist and her teaching on the eucharistic sacrifice have both been the subject in recent decades of a fruitful dialogue *in the area of ecumenism*. We must give thanks to the Blessed Trinity for the significant progress and convergence achieved in this regard, which lead us to hope one day for a full sharing of faith. Nonetheless, the observations of the Council concerning the ecclesial communities which arose in the West from the sixteenth century onwards and are separated from the Catholic Church remain fully pertinent: "The ecclesial communities separated from us lack that fullness of unity with us which should flow from baptism, and we believe that especially because of the lack of the sacrament of Orders they have not preserved the genuine and total reality of the eucharistic mystery. Nevertheless, when they commemorate the Lord's death and resurrection in the Holy Supper, they profess that it signifies life in communion with Christ and they await his coming in glory."[62]

The Catholic faithful, therefore, while respecting the religious convictions of these separated brethren, must refrain from receiving the Communion distributed in their celebrations, so as not to condone an ambiguity about the nature of the Eucharist and, consequently, to fail in their duty to bear clear witness to the truth. This would result in slowing the progress being made toward full visible unity. Similarly, it is unthinkable to substitute for Sunday Mass ecumenical celebrations of the word or services of common prayer with Christians from the aforementioned ecclesial communities, or even participation in their own liturgical services. Such celebrations and services, however praiseworthy in certain situations, prepare for the goal of full communion, including eucharistic Communion, but they cannot replace it.

The fact that the power of consecrating the Eucharist has been entrusted only to Bishops and priests does not represent any kind of belittlement of the rest of the People of God, for in the Communion of the one body of Christ, which is the Church, this gift redounds to the benefit of all.

31. If the Eucharist is the center and summit of the Church's life, it is likewise the center and summit of priestly ministry. For this reason, with a heart filled with gratitude to our Lord Jesus Christ, I repeat that the Eucharist "is the principal and central *raison d'être* of the sacrament of priesthood, which effectively came into being at the moment of the institution of the Eucharist."[63]

Priests are engaged in a wide variety of pastoral activities. If we also consider the social and cultural conditions of the modern world, it is easy to understand how priests face the very real *risk of losing their focus* amid such a great number of different tasks. The Second Vatican Council saw in pastoral charity the bond which gives unity to the priest's life and work. This, the Council adds, "flows mainly from the eucharistic sacrifice, which is therefore the center and root of the whole priestly life."[64] We can understand, then, how important it is for the spiritual life of the priest, as well as for the good of the Church and the world, that priests follow the Council's recommendation to celebrate the Eucharist daily: "for even if the faithful are unable to be present, it is an act of Christ and the Church."[65] In this way priests will be able to counteract the daily tensions which lead to a lack of focus and they will find in the eucharistic sacrifice-the true center of their lives and ministry—the spiritual strength needed to deal with their different pastoral responsibilities. Their daily activity will thus become truly eucharistic.

The centrality of the Eucharist in the life and ministry of priests is the basis of its centrality in the *pastoral promotion of priestly vocations*. It is in the Eucharist that prayer for vocations is most closely united to the prayer of Christ the Eternal High Priest. At the same time, the diligence of priests in carrying out their eucharistic ministry, together with the conscious, active and fruitful participation of the faithful in the Eucharist, provides young men with a powerful example and incentive for responding generously to God's call. Often it is the example of a priest's fervent pastoral charity which the Lord uses to sow and to bring to fruition in a young man's heart the seed of a priestly calling.

32. All of this shows how distressing and irregular is the situation of a Christian community which, despite having sufficient numbers and variety of faithful to form a parish, does not have a priest to lead it. Parishes are communities of the baptized who express and affirm their identity above all through the celebration of the eucharistic sacrifice. But this requires the presence of a presbyter, who alone is qualified to offer the Eucharist *in persona Christi*. When a community lacks a priest, attempts are rightly made somehow to remedy the situation so that it can continue its Sunday celebrations, and those religious and laity who lead their brothers and sisters in prayer exercise in a praiseworthy way the common priesthood of all the faithful based on the grace of baptism. But such solutions must be considered merely temporary, while the community awaits a priest.

The sacramental incompleteness of these celebrations should above all inspire the whole community to pray with greater fervor that the Lord will send laborers into his harvest (cf. *Mt* 9:38). It should also be an incentive to mobilize all the resources needed for an adequate pastoral promotion of vocations, without yielding to the temptation to seek solutions which lower the moral and formative standards demanded of candidates for the priesthood.

33. When, due to the scarcity of priests, non-ordained members of the faithful are entrusted with a share in the pastoral care of a parish, they should bear in mind that-as the Second Vatican Council teaches-"no Christian community can be built up unless it has its basis and center the celebration of the most Holy Eucharist."[66] They have a responsibility, therefore, to keep alive in the community a genuine "hunger" for the Eucharist, so that no opportunity for the celebration of Mass will ever be missed, also taking advantage of the occasional presence of a priest who is not impeded by Church law from celebrating Mass.

CHAPTER FOUR

THE EUCHARIST AND ECCLESIAL COMMUNION

34. The Extraordinary Assembly of the Synod of Bishops in 1985 saw in the concept of an "ecclesiology of communion" the central and fundamental idea of the documents of the Second Vatican Council.[67] The Church is called during her earthly pilgrimage to maintain and promote communion with the Triune God and communion among the faithful. For this purpose she possesses the word and the sacraments, particularly the Eucharist, by which she "constantly lives and grows"[68] and in which she expresses her very nature. It is not by chance that the term *communion* has become one of the names given to this sublime sacrament.

The Eucharist thus appears as the culmination of all the sacraments in perfecting our communion with God the Father by identification with his only-begotten Son through the working of the Holy Spirit. With discerning faith, a distinguished writer of the Byzantine tradition voiced this truth: in the Eucharist "unlike any other sacrament, the mystery [of Communion] is so perfect that it brings us to the heights of every good thing: here is the ultimate goal of every human desire, because here we attain God and God joins himself to us in the most perfect union."[69] Precisely for this reason it is good to *cultivate in our hearts a constant desire for the sacrament of the Eucharist*. This was the origin of the practice of "spiritual communion," which has happily been established in the Church for centuries and recommended by saints who were masters of the spiritual life. Saint Teresa of Jesus wrote: "When you do not receive Communion and you do not attend Mass, you can make a spiritual communion, which is a most beneficial practice; by it the love of God will be greatly impressed on you."[70]

35. The celebration of the Eucharist, however, cannot be the starting point for communion; it presupposes that communion already exists, a communion which it seeks to consolidate and bring to perfection. The sacrament is an expression of this bond of communion both in its *invisible* dimension, which, in Christ and through the working of the Holy Spirit, unites us to the Father and among ourselves, and in its *visible* dimension, which entails communion in the teaching of the Apostles, in the sacraments and in the Church's hierarchical order. The profound relationship between the invisible and the visible elements of ecclesial communion is constitutive of the Church as the sacrament of salvation.[71] Only in this context can there be a legitimate celebration of the Eucharist and true participation in it. Consequently it is an intrinsic requirement of the Eucharist that it should be celebrated in communion, and specifically maintaining the various bonds of that communion intact.

36. Invisible communion, though by its nature always growing, presupposes the life of grace, by which we become "partakers of the divine nature" (*2 Pet* 1:4), and the practice of the virtues of faith, hope and love. Only in this way do we have true communion with the Father, the Son and the Holy Spirit. Nor is faith sufficient; we must persevere in sanctifying grace and love, remaining within the Church "bodily" as well as "in our heart";[72] what is required, in the words of Saint Paul, is "faith working through love" (*Gal* 5:6).

Keeping these invisible bonds intact is a specific moral duty incumbent upon Christians who wish to participate fully in the Eucharist by receiving the body and blood of Christ. The Apostle Paul appeals to this duty when he warns: "Let a man examine himself, and so eat of the bread and drink of the cup" (*1 Cor* 11:28). Saint John Chrysostom, with his stirring eloquence, exhorted the faithful: "I too raise my voice, I beseech, beg and implore that no one draw near to this sacred table with a sullied and corrupt conscience. Such an act, in fact, can never be called 'communion,' not even were we to touch the Lord's body a thousand times over, but 'condemnation,' 'torment' and 'increase of punishment.'"[73]

Along these same lines, the *Catechism of the Catholic Church* rightly stipulates that "anyone conscious of a grave sin must receive the sacrament of Reconciliation before coming to Communion."[74] I therefore desire to reaffirm that in the Church there remains in force, now and in the future, the rule by which the Council of Trent gave concrete expression to the Apostle Paul's stern warning when it affirmed that, in order to receive the Eucharist in a worthy manner, "one must first confess one's sins, when one is aware of mortal sin."[75]

37. The two sacraments of the Eucharist and Penance are very closely connected. Because the Eucharist makes present the redeeming sacrifice of the cross, perpetuating it sacramentally, it naturally gives rise to a continuous need for conversion, for a personal response to the appeal made by Saint Paul to the Christians of Corinth: "We beseech you on behalf of Christ, be reconciled to God" (*2 Cor* 5:20). If a Christian's conscience is burdened by serious sin, then the path of penance through the sacrament of Reconciliation becomes necessary for full participation in the eucharistic sacrifice.

The judgment of one's state of grace obviously belongs only to the person involved, since it is a question of examining one's conscience. However, in cases of outward conduct which is seriously, clearly and steadfastly contrary to the moral norm, the Church, in her pastoral concern for the good order of the community and out of respect for the sacrament, cannot fail to feel directly involved. The *Code of Canon Law* refers to this situation of a manifest lack of proper moral disposition when it states that those who "obstinately persist in manifest grave sin" are not to be admitted to eucharistic Communion.[76]

38. Ecclesial communion, as I have said, is likewise *visible*, and finds expression in the series of "bonds" listed by the Council when it teaches: "They are fully incorporated into the society of the Church who, possessing the Spirit of Christ, accept her whole structure and all the means of salvation established within her, and within her visible framework are united to Christ, who governs her through the Supreme Pontiff and the Bishops, by the bonds of profession of faith, the sacraments, ecclesiastical government and communion."[77]

The Eucharist, as the supreme sacramental manifestation of communion in the Church, demands to be celebrated in *a context where the outward bonds of communion are also intact*. In a special way, since the Eucharist is "as it were the summit of the spiritual life and the goal of all the sacraments,"[78] it requires that the bonds of communion in the sacraments, particularly in baptism and in priestly orders, be real. It is not possible to give Communion to a person who is not baptized or to one who rejects the full truth of the faith regarding the eucharistic mystery. Christ is the truth and he bears witness to the truth (cf. *Jn* 14:6; 18:37); the sacrament of his body and blood does not permit duplicity.

39. Furthermore, given the very nature of ecclesial communion and its relation to the sacrament of the Eucharist, it must be recalled that "the eucharistic sacrifice, while always offered in a particular community, is never a celebration of that community alone. In fact, the community, in receiving the eucharistic presence of the Lord, receives the entire gift of salvation and shows, even in its lasting visible particular form, that it is the image and true presence of the one, holy, catholic and apostolic Church."[79] From this it follows that a truly eucharistic community cannot be closed in upon itself, as though it were somehow self-sufficient; rather it must persevere in harmony with every other Catholic community.

The ecclesial communion of the eucharistic assembly is a communion with its own *Bishop* and with the *Roman Pontiff*. The Bishop, in effect, is the visible principle and the foundation of unity within his particular church.[80] It would therefore be a great contradiction if the sacrament par excellence of the Church's unity were celebrated without true communion with the Bishop. As Saint Ignatius of Antioch wrote: "That Eucharist which is celebrated under the Bishop, or under one to whom the Bishop has given this charge, may be considered certain."[81] Likewise, since "the Roman Pontiff, as the successor of Peter, is the perpetual and visible source and foundation of the unity of the Bishops and of the multitude of the faithful,"[82] communion with him is intrinsically required for the celebration of the eucharistic sacrifice. Hence the great truth expressed which the Liturgy expresses in a variety of ways: "Every celebration of the Eucharist is performed in union not only with the proper Bishop, but also with the Pope, with the episcopal order, with all the clergy, and with the entire people. Every valid celebration of the Eucharist expresses this universal communion with Peter and with the whole Church, or objectively calls for it, as in the case of the Christian Churches separated from Rome."[83]

40. The Eucharist *creates communion* and *fosters communion*. Saint Paul wrote to the faithful of Corinth explaining how their divisions, reflected in their eucharistic gatherings, contradicted what they were celebrating, the Lord's Supper. The Apostle then urged them to reflect on the true reality of the Eucharist in order to return to the spirit of fraternal communion (cf. *1 Cor* 11:17-34). Saint Augustine effectively echoed this call when, in recalling the Apostle's words: "You are the body of Christ and individually members of it" (*1 Cor* 12: 27), he went on to say: "If you are his body and members of him, then you will find set on the Lord's table your own mystery. Yes, you receive your own mystery."[84] And from this observation, he concludes: "Christ the Lord ... hallowed at his table the mystery of our peace and unity. Whoever receives the mystery of unity without preserving the bonds of peace receives not a mystery for his benefit but evidence against himself."[85]

41. The Eucharist's particular effectiveness in promoting communion is one of the reasons for the importance of Sunday Mass. I have already dwelled on this and on the other reasons which make Sunday Mass fundamental for the life of the Church and of individual believers in my apostolic letter on the sanctification of Sunday *Dies Domini*.[86] There I recalled that the faithful have the obligation to attend Mass, unless they are seriously impeded, and that pastors have the corresponding duty to see that it is practical and possible for all to fulfill this precept.[87] More recently, in my apostolic letter *Novo Millennio Ineunte*, in setting forth the pastoral path which the Church must take at the beginning of the third millennium, I drew particular attention to the Sunday Eucharist, emphasizing its effectiveness for building communion. "It is"-I wrote-"the privileged place where communion is ceaselessly proclaimed and nurtured. Precisely through sharing in the Eucharist, *the Lord's Day* also becomes *the Day of the Church*, when she can effectively exercise her role as the sacrament of unity."[88]

42. The safeguarding and promotion of ecclesial communion is a task of each member of the faithful, who finds in the Eucharist, as the sacrament of the Church's unity, an area of special concern. More specifically, this task is the particular responsibility of the Church's pastors, each according to his rank and ecclesiastical office. For this reason the Church has drawn up norms aimed both at fostering the frequent and fruitful access of the faithful to the eucharistic table and at determining the objective conditions under which Communion may not be given. The care shown in promoting the faithful observance of these norms becomes a practical means of showing love for the Eucharist and for the Church.

43. In considering the Eucharist as the sacrament of ecclesial communion, there is one subject which, due to its importance, must not be overlooked: I am referring to the *relationship of the Eucharist to ecumenical activity*. We should all give thanks to the Blessed Trinity for the many members of the faithful throughout the world who in recent decades have felt an ardent desire for unity among all Christians. The Second Vatican Council, at the beginning of its Decree on Ecumenism, sees this as a special gift of God.[89] It was an efficacious grace which inspired us, the sons and daughters of the Catholic Church and our brothers and sisters from other churches and ecclesial communities, to set forth on the path of ecumenism.

Our longing for the goal of unity prompts us to turn to the Eucharist, which is the supreme sacrament of the unity of the People of God, in as much as it is the apt expression and the unsurpassable source of that unity.[90] In the celebration of the eucharistic sacrifice, the Church prays that God, the Father of mercies, will grant his children the fullness of the Holy Spirit so that they may become one body and one spirit in Christ.[91] In raising this prayer to the Father of lights, from whom comes every good endowment and every perfect gift (cf. *Jas*

1:17), the Church believes that she will be heard, for she prays in union with Christ her Head and Spouse, who takes up this plea of his Bride and joins it to that of his own redemptive sacrifice

44. Precisely because the Church's unity, which the Eucharist brings about through the Lord's sacrifice and by communion in his body and blood, absolutely requires full communion in the bonds of the profession of faith, the sacraments and ecclesiastical governance, it is not possible to celebrate together the same eucharistic liturgy until those bonds are fully re-established. Any such concelebration would not be a valid means, and might well prove instead to be *an obstacle, to the attainment of full communion*, by weakening the sense of how far we remain from this goal and by introducing or exacerbating ambiguities with regard to one or another truth of the faith. The path toward full unity can only be undertaken in truth. In this area, the prohibitions of Church law leave no room for uncertainty,[92] in fidelity to the moral norm laid down by the Second Vatican Council.[93]

I would like nonetheless to reaffirm what I said in my encyclical letter *Ut Unum Sint* after having acknowledged the impossibility of eucharistic sharing: "And yet we do have a burning desire to join in celebrating the one Eucharist of the Lord, and this desire itself is already a common prayer of praise, a single supplication. Together we speak to the Father and increasingly we do so 'with one heart.'"[94]

45. While it is never legitimate to concelebrate in the absence of full communion, the same is not true with respect to the administration of the Eucharist *under special circumstances, to individual persons* belonging to churches or ecclesial communities not in full communion with the Catholic Church. In this case, in fact, the intention is to meet a grave spiritual need for the eternal salvation of an individual believer, not to bring about an *intercommunion* which remains impossible until the visible bonds of ecclesial communion are fully re-established.

This was the approach taken by the Second Vatican Council when it gave guidelines for responding to Eastern Christians separated in good faith from the Catholic Church, who spontaneously ask to receive the Eucharist from a Catholic minister and are properly disposed.[95] This approach was then ratified by both Codes, which also consider-with necessary modifications-the case of other non-Eastern Christians who are not in full communion with the Catholic Church.[96]

46. In my encyclical *Ut Unum Sint* I expressed my own appreciation of these norms, which make it possible to provide for the salvation of souls with proper discernment: "It is a source of joy to note that Catholic ministers are able, in certain particular cases, to administer the sacraments of the Eucharist, Penance and Anointing of the Sick to Christians who are not in full communion with the Catholic Church but who greatly desire to receive these sacraments, freely request them and manifest the faith which the Catholic Church professes with regard to these sacraments. Conversely, in specific cases and in particular circumstances, Catholics too can request these same sacraments from ministers of Churches in which these sacraments are valid."[97]

These conditions, from which no dispensation can be given, must be carefully respected, even though they deal with specific individual cases, because the denial of one or more truths of the faith regarding these sacraments and, among these, the truth regarding the need of the ministerial priesthood for their validity, renders the person asking improperly disposed to legitimately receiving them. And the opposite is also true: Catholics may not receive Communion in those communities which lack a valid sacrament of Holy Orders.[98]

The faithful observance of the body of norms established in this area[99] is a manifestation and, at the same time, a guarantee of our love for Jesus Christ in the Blessed Sacrament, for our brothers and sisters of different Christian confessions-who have a right to our witness to the truth-and for the cause itself of the promotion of unity.

CHAPTER FIVE
THE DIGNITY OF THE EUCHARISTIC CELEBRATION

47. Reading the account of the institution of the Eucharist in the Synoptic Gospels, we are struck by the simplicity and the solemnity with which Jesus, on the evening of the Last Supper, instituted this great sacrament. There is an episode which in some way serves as its prelude: *the anointing at Bethany*. A woman, whom John identifies as Mary the sister of Lazarus, pours a flask of *costly ointment* over Jesus' head, which provokes from the disciples-and from Judas in particular (cf. *Mt* 26:8; *Mk* 14:4; *Jn* 12:4)-an indignant response, as if this act, in light of the needs of the poor, represented an intolerable "waste." But Jesus' own reaction is completely different. While in no way detracting from the duty of charity toward the needy, for whom the disciples must always show special care—"the poor you will always have with you" (*Mt* 26:11; *Mk* 14:7; cf. *Jn* 12:8), he looks toward his imminent death and burial, and sees this act of anointing as an anticipation of the honor which his body will continue to merit even after his death, indissolubly bound as it is to the mystery of his person.

The account continues, in the Synoptic Gospels, with Jesus' charge to the disciples to *prepare carefully the "large upper room"* needed for the Passover meal (cf. *Mk* 14:15; *Lk* 22:12) and with the narration of the institution of the Eucharist. Reflecting at least in part the *Jewish rites* of the Passover meal leading up to the singing of the Hallel (cf. *Mt* 26:30; *Mk* 14:26), the story presents with sobriety and solemnity, even in the variants of the different traditions, the words spoken by Christ over the bread and wine, which he made into concrete expressions of the handing over of his body and the shedding of his blood. All these details are recorded by the Evangelists in the light of a praxis of the "breaking of the bread" already well-established in the early Church. But certainly from the time of Jesus on, the event of Holy Thursday has shown visible traces of a liturgical "sensibility" shaped by Old Testament tradition and open to being reshaped in Christian celebrations in a way consonant with the new content of Easter.

48. Like the woman who anointed Jesus in Bethany, *the Church has feared no "extravagance,"* devoting the best of her resources to expressing her wonder and adoration before the *unsurpassable gift of the Eucharist.* No less than the first disciples charged with preparing the "large upper room," she has felt the need, down the centuries and in her encounters with different cultures, to celebrate the Eucharist in a setting worthy of so great a mystery. In the wake of Jesus' own words and actions, and building upon the ritual heritage of Judaism, the *Christian liturgy was born.* Could there ever be an adequate means of expressing the acceptance of that self-gift which the divine Bridegroom continually makes to his Bride, the Church, by bringing the sacrifice offered once and for all on the cross to successive generations of believers and thus becoming nourishment for all the faithful? Though the idea of a "banquet" naturally suggests familiarity, the Church has never yielded to the temptation to trivialize this "intimacy" with her Spouse by forgetting that he is also her Lord and that the "banquet" always remains a sacrificial banquet marked by the blood shed on Golgotha. *The eucharistic banquet is truly a "sacred" banquet*, in which the simplicity of the signs conceals the unfathomable holiness of God: *O sacrum convivium, in quo Christus sumitur!* The bread which is broken on our altars, offered to us as wayfarers along the paths of the world, is *panis angelorum*, the bread of angels, which cannot be approached except with the humility of the centurion in the Gospel: "Lord, I am not worthy to have you come under my roof " (*Mt* 8:8; *Lk* 7:6).

49. With this heightened sense of mystery, we understand how the faith of the Church in the mystery of the Eucharist has found historical expression not only in the demand for an interior disposition of devotion, but also in *outward forms* meant to evoke and emphasize the grandeur of the event being celebrated. This led progressively to the development of a *particular form of regulating the eucharistic liturgy,* with due respect for the various legitimately constituted ecclesial traditions. On this foundation *a rich artistic heritage* also developed. Architecture, sculpture, painting and music, moved by the Christian mystery, have found in the Eucharist, both directly and indirectly, a source of great inspiration.

Such was the case, for example, with architecture, which witnessed the transition, once the historical situation made it possible, from the first places of eucharistic celebration in the *domus* or "homes" of Christian families to the solemn *basilicas* of the early centuries, to the imposing *cathedrals* of the Middle Ages, and to the *churches*, large and small, which gradually sprang up throughout the lands touched by Christianity. The designs of altars and tabernacles within Church interiors were often not simply motivated by artistic inspiration but also by a clear understanding of the mystery. The same could be said for *sacred music* if we but think of the inspired Gregorian melodies and the many, often great, composers who sought to do justice to the liturgical texts of the Mass. Similarly, can we overlook the enormous quantity of *artistic production*, ranging from fine craftsmanship to authentic works of art, in the area of Church furnishings and vestments used for the celebration of the Eucharist?

It can be said that the Eucharist, while shaping the Church and her spirituality, has also powerfully affected "culture," and the arts in particular.

50. In this effort to adore the mystery grasped in its ritual and aesthetic dimensions, a certain "competition" has taken place between Christians of the West and the East. How could we not give particular thanks to the Lord for the contributions to Christian art made by the great architectural and artistic works of the Greco-Byzantine tradition and of the whole geographical area marked by Slav culture? In the East, sacred art has preserved a remarkably powerful sense of mystery, which leads artists to see their efforts at creating beauty not simply as an expression of their own talents, but also as a *genuine service to the faith*. Passing well beyond mere technical skill, they have shown themselves docile and open to the inspiration of the Holy Spirit.

The architectural and mosaic splendors of the Christian East and West are a patrimony belonging to all believers; they contain a hope, and even a pledge, of the desired fullness of communion in faith and in celebration. This would presuppose and demand, as in Rublëv's famous depiction of the Trinity, *a profoundly eucharistic Church* in which the presence of the mystery of Christ in the broken bread is as it were immersed in the ineffable unity of the three divine Persons, making of the Church herself an "icon" of the Trinity.

Within this context of an art aimed at expressing, in all its elements, the meaning of the Eucharist in accordance with the Church's teaching, attention needs to be given to the norms regulating *the construction and decor of sacred buildings*. As history shows and as I emphasized in my *Letter to Artists,*[100] the Church has always left ample room for the creativity of artists. But sacred art must be outstanding for its ability to express adequately the mystery grasped in the fullness of the Church's faith and in accordance with the pastoral guidelines appropriately laid down by competent Authority. This holds true both for the figurative arts and for sacred music.

51. The development of sacred art and liturgical discipline which took place in lands of ancient Christian heritage is also taking place *on continents where Christianity is younger.* This was precisely the approach supported by the Second Vatican Council on the need for sound and proper "enculturation." In my numerous Pastoral Visits, I have seen, throughout the world, the great vitality which the celebration of the Eucharist can have when marked by the forms, styles and sensibilities of different cultures. By adaptation to the changing conditions of time and place, the Eucharist offers sustenance not only to individuals but to entire peoples, and it shapes cultures inspired by Christianity.

It is necessary, however, that this important work of adaptation be carried out with a constant awareness of the ineffable mystery against which every generation is called to measure itself. The "treasure" is too important and precious to risk impoverishment or compromise through forms of experimentation or practices introduced without a careful review on the part of the competent ecclesiastical authorities. Furthermore, the centrality of the eucharistic mystery demands that any such review must be undertaken in close association with the Holy See. As I wrote in my post-synodal apostolic exhortation *Ecclesia in Asia,* "such cooperation is essential because the sacred liturgy expresses and celebrates the one faith professed by all and, being the heritage of the whole Church, cannot be determined by local churches in isolation from the universal Church."[101]

52. All of this makes clear the great responsibility which belongs to priests in particular for the celebration of the Eucharist. It is their responsibility to preside at the Eucharist *in persona Christi* and to provide a witness to and a service of communion not only for the community directly taking part in the celebration, but also for the universal Church, which is a part of every Eucharist. It must be lamented that, especially in the years following the post-conciliar liturgical reform, as a result of a misguided sense of creativity and adaptation, there have been a number of abuses which have been a source of suffering for many. A certain reaction against "formalism" has led some, especially in certain regions, to consider the "forms" chosen by the Church's great liturgical tradition and her Magisterium as non-binding and to introduce unauthorized innovations which are often completely inappropriate.

I consider it my duty, therefore, to appeal urgently that the liturgical norms for the celebration of the Eucharist be observed with great fidelity. These norms are a concrete expression of the authentically ecclesial nature of the Eucharist; this is their deepest meaning. Liturgy is never anyone's private property, be it of the celebrant or of the community in which the mysteries are celebrated. The Apostle Paul had to address fiery words to the community of Corinth because of grave shortcomings in their celebration of the Eucharist resulting in divisions (*schismata*) and the emergence of factions (*haireseis*) (cf. *1 Cor* 11:17-34). Our time, too, calls for a renewed awareness and appreciation of liturgical norms as a reflection of, and a witness to, the one universal Church made present in every celebration of the Eucharist. Priests who faithfully celebrate Mass according to the liturgical norms, and communities which conform to those norms, quietly but eloquently demonstrate their love for the Church. Precisely to bring out more clearly this deeper meaning of liturgical norms, I have asked the competent offices of the Roman Curia to prepare a more specific document, including prescriptions of a juridical nature, on this very important subject. No one is permitted to undervalue the mystery entrusted to our hands: it is too great for anyone to feel free to treat it lightly and with disregard for its sacredness and its universality.

CHAPTER SIX
AT THE SCHOOL OF MARY, "WOMAN OF THE EUCHARIST"

53. If we wish to rediscover in all its richness the profound relationship between the Church and the Eucharist, we cannot neglect Mary, Mother and model of the Church. In my apostolic letter *Rosarium Virginis Mariae*, I pointed to the Blessed Virgin Mary as our teacher in contemplating Christ's face, and among the mysteries of light I included *the institution of the Eucharist*.[102] Mary can guide us toward this most holy sacrament, because she herself has a profound relationship with it.

At first glance, the Gospel is silent on this subject. The account of the institution of the Eucharist on the night of Holy Thursday makes no mention of Mary. Yet we know that she was present among the Apostles who prayed "with one accord" (cf. *Acts* 1:14) *in the first community which gathered after the Ascension in expectation of Pentecost*. Certainly Mary must have been present at the eucharistic celebrations of the first generation of Christians, who were devoted to "the breaking of bread" (*Acts* 2:42).

But in addition to her sharing in the eucharistic banquet, an indirect picture of Mary's relationship with the Eucharist can be had, beginning with her interior disposition. Mary is a *"woman of the Eucharist" in her whole life*. The Church, which looks to Mary as a model, is also called to imitate her in her relationship with this most holy mystery.

54. *Mysterium fidei!* If the Eucharist is a mystery of faith which so greatly transcends our understanding as to call for sheer abandonment to the word of God, then there can be no one like Mary to act as our support and guide in acquiring this disposition. In repeating what Christ did at the Last Supper in obedience to his command: "Do this in memory of me!" we also accept Mary's invitation to obey him without hesitation: "Do whatever he tells you" (*Jn* 2:5). With the same maternal concern which she showed at the wedding feast of Cana, Mary seems to say to us: "Do not waver; trust in the words of my Son. If he was able to change water into wine, he can also turn bread and wine into his body and blood, and through this mystery bestow on believers the living memorial of his Passover, thus becoming the 'bread of life.'"

55. In a certain sense Mary lived her *eucharistic faith* even before the institution of the Eucharist, by the very fact that *she offered her virginal womb for the incarnation of God's Word*. The Eucharist, while commemorating the passion and resurrection, is also in continuity with the incarnation. At the Annunciation, Mary conceived the Son of God in the physical reality of his body and blood, thus anticipating within herself what to some degree happens sacramentally in every believer who receives, under the signs of bread and wine, the Lord's body and blood.

As a result, there is a profound analogy between the Fiat which Mary said in reply to the angel, and the *Amen* which every believer says when receiving the body of the Lord. Mary was asked to believe that the One whom she conceived "through the Holy Spirit" was "the Son of God" (*Lk* 1:30-35). In continuity with the Virgin's faith, in the eucharistic mystery we are asked to believe that the same Jesus Christ, Son of God and Son of Mary, becomes present in his full humanity and divinity under the signs of bread and wine.

"Blessed is she who believed" (*Lk* 1:45). Mary also anticipated, in the mystery of the incarnation, the Church's eucharistic faith. When, at the Visitation, she bore in her womb the Word made flesh, she became in some way a "tabernacle"—the first "tabernacle" in history—in which the Son of God, still invisible to our human gaze, allowed himself to be adored by Elizabeth, radiating his light as it were through the eyes and the voice of Mary. And is not the enraptured gaze of Mary as she contemplated the face of the newborn Christ and cradled him in her arms that unparalleled model of love which should inspire us every time we receive eucharistic Communion?

56. Mary, throughout her life at Christ's side and not only on Calvary, made her own *the sacrificial dimension of the Eucharist.* When she brought the child Jesus to the Temple in Jerusalem "to present him to the Lord" (*Lk* 2:22), she heard the aged Simeon announce that the child would be a "sign of contradiction" and that a sword would also pierce her own heart (cf. *Lk* 2:34-35). The tragedy of her Son's crucifixion was thus foretold, and in some sense, Mary's Stabat Mater at the foot of the cross was foreshadowed. In her daily preparation for Calvary, Mary experienced a kind of "anticipated Eucharist"-one might say a "spiritual communion"-of desire and of oblation, which would culminate in her union with her Son in his passion, and then find expression after Easter by her partaking in the Eucharist which the Apostles celebrated as the memorial of that passion.

What must Mary have felt as she heard from the mouth of Peter, John, James and the other Apostles the words spoken at the Last Supper: "This is my body which is given for you" (*Lk* 22:19)? The body given up for us and made present under sacramental signs was the same body which she had conceived in her womb! For Mary, receiving the Eucharist must have somehow meant welcoming once more into her womb that heart which had beat in unison with hers and reliving what she had experienced at the foot of the cross.

57. "Do this in remembrance of me" (*Lk* 22:19). In the "memorial" of Calvary all that Christ accomplished by his passion and his death is present. Consequently *all that Christ did with regard to his Mother* for our sake is also present. To her he gave the beloved disciple and, in him, each of us: "Behold, your Son!" To each of us he also says: "Behold your mother!" (cf. *Jn* 19: 26-27).

Experiencing the memorial of Christ's death in the Eucharist also means continually receiving this gift. It means accepting-like John-the one who is given to us anew as our Mother. It also means taking on a commitment to be conformed to Christ, putting ourselves at the school of his Mother and allowing her to accompany us. Mary is present, with the Church and as the Mother of the Church, at each of our celebrations of the Eucharist. If the Church and the Eucharist are inseparably united, the same ought to be said of Mary and the Eucharist. This is one reason why, since ancient times, the commemoration of Mary has always been part of the eucharistic celebrations of the Churches of East and West.

58. In the Eucharist, the Church is completely united to Christ and his sacrifice and makes her own the spirit of Mary. This truth can be understood more deeply by *re-reading the Magnificat* in a eucharistic key. The Eucharist, like the Canticle of Mary, is first and foremost praise and thanksgiving. When Mary exclaims: "My soul magnifies the Lord and my spirit rejoices in God my Savior," she already bears Jesus in her womb. She praises God "through" Jesus, but she also praises him "in" Jesus and "with" Jesus. This is itself the true "eucharistic attitude."

At the same time, Mary recalls the wonders worked by God in salvation history in fulfillment of the promise once made to the fathers (cf. *Lk* 1:55), and proclaims the wonder that surpasses them all, the redemptive incarnation. Lastly, the *Magnificat* reflects the eschatological tension of the Eucharist. Every time the Son of God comes again to us in the "poverty" of the sacramental signs of bread and wine, the seeds of that new history wherein the mighty are "put down from their thrones" and "those of low degree are exalted" (cf. *Lk* 1:52), take root in the world. Mary sings of the "new heavens" and the "new earth" which find in the Eucharist their anticipation and in some sense their program and plan. The *Magnificat* expresses Mary's spirituality, and there is nothing greater than this spirituality for helping us to experience the mystery of the Eucharist. The Eucharist has been given to us so that our life, like that of Mary, may become completely a *Magnificat!*

CONCLUSION

59. *Ave, verum corpus natum de Maria Virgine!* Several years ago I celebrated the fiftieth anniversary of my priesthood. Today I have the grace of offering the Church this encyclical on the Eucharist on the Holy Thursday which falls *during the twenty-fifth year of my Petrine ministry.* As I do so, my heart is filled with gratitude. For over a half century, every day, beginning on 2 November 1946, when I celebrated my first Mass in the Crypt of Saint Leonard in Wawel Cathedral in Krakow, my eyes have gazed in recollection upon the host and the chalice, where time and space in some way "merge" and the drama of Golgotha is re-presented in a living way, thus revealing its mysterious "contemporaneity." Each day my faith has been able to recognize in the consecrated bread and wine the divine Wayfarer who joined the two disciples on the road to Emmaus and opened their eyes to the light and their hearts to new hope (cf. *Lk* 24:13-35).

Allow me, dear brothers and sisters, to share with deep emotion, as a means of accompanying and strengthening your faith, my own testimony of faith in the Most Holy Eucharist. *Ave verum corpus natum de Maria Virgine, vere passum, immolatum, in cruce pro homine!* Here is the Church's treasure, the heart of the world, the pledge of the fulfillment for which each man and woman, even unconsciously, yearns. A great and transcendent mystery, indeed, and one that taxes our mind's ability to pass beyond appearances. Here our senses fail us: *visus, tactus, gustus in te fallitur,* in the words of the hymn *Adoro Te Devote;* yet faith alone, rooted in the word of Christ handed down to us by the Apostles, is sufficient for us. Allow me, like Peter at the end of the eucharistic discourse in John's Gospel, to say once more to Christ, in the name of the whole Church and in the name of each of you: "Lord to whom shall we go? You have the words of eternal life" (*Jn* 6:68).

60. At the dawn of this third millennium, we, the children of the Church, are called to undertake with renewed enthusiasm the journey of Christian living. As I wrote in my apostolic letter *Novo Millennio Ineunte*, "it is not a matter of inventing a 'new program.' The program already exists: it is the plan found in the Gospel and in the living Tradition; it is the same as ever. Ultimately, it has its center in Christ himself, who is to be known, loved and imitated, so that in him we may live the life of the Trinity, and with him transform history until its fulfillment in the heavenly Jerusalem."[103] The implementation of this program of a renewed impetus in Christian living passes through the Eucharist.

Every commitment to holiness, every activity aimed at carrying out the Church's mission, every work of pastoral planning, must draw the strength it needs from the eucharistic mystery and in turn be directed to that mystery as its culmination. In the Eucharist we have Jesus, we have his redemptive sacrifice, we have his resurrection, we have the gift of the Holy Spirit, we have adoration, obedience and love of the Father. Were we to disregard the Eucharist, how could we overcome our own deficiency?

61. The mystery of the Eucharist—sacrifice, presence, banquet—*does not allow for reduction or exploitation;* it must be experienced and lived in its integrity, both in its celebration and in the intimate converse with Jesus which takes place after receiving Communion or in a prayerful moment of eucharistic adoration apart from Mass. These are times when the Church is firmly built up and it becomes clear what she truly is: one, holy, catholic and apostolic; the people, temple and family of God; the body and bride of Christ, enlivened by the Holy Spirit; the universal sacrament of salvation and a hierarchically structured communion.

The path taken by the Church in these first years of the third millennium is also a *path of renewed ecumenical commitment.* The final decades of the second millennium, culminating in the Great Jubilee, have spurred us along this path and called for all the baptized to respond to the prayer of Jesus *"ut unum sint"* (*Jn* 17:11). The path itself is long and strewn with obstacles greater than our human resources alone can overcome, yet we have the Eucharist, and in its presence we can hear in the depths of our hearts, as if they were addressed to us, the same words heard by the Prophet Elijah: "Arise and eat, else the journey will be too great for you" (*1 Kg* 19:7). The treasure of the Eucharist, which the Lord places before us, impels us toward the goal of full sharing with all our brothers and sisters to whom we are joined by our common baptism. But if this treasure is not to be squandered, we need to respect the demands which derive from its being the sacrament of communion in faith and in apostolic succession.

By giving the Eucharist the prominence it deserves, and by being careful not to diminish any of its dimensions or demands, we show that we are truly conscious of the greatness of this gift. We are urged to do so by an uninterrupted tradition, which from the first centuries on has found the Christian community ever vigilant in guarding this "treasure." Inspired by love, the Church is anxious to hand on to future generations of Christians, without loss, her faith and teaching with regard to the mystery of the Eucharist. There can be no danger of excess in our care for this mystery, for "in this sacrament is recapitulated the whole mystery of our salvation."[104]

62. Let us take our place, dear brothers and sisters, *at the school of the saints,* who are the great interpreters of true eucharistic piety. In them the theology of the Eucharist takes on all the splendor of a lived reality; it becomes "contagious" and, in a manner of speaking, it "warms our hearts." Above all, let us *listen to Mary Most Holy,* in whom the mystery of the Eucharist appears, more than in anyone else, as a *mystery of light.* Gazing upon Mary, we come to know *the transforming power present in the Eucharist.* In her we see the world renewed in love. Contemplating her, assumed body and soul into heaven, we see opening up before us those "new heavens" and that "new earth" which will appear at the second coming of Christ. Here below, the Eucharist represents their pledge, and in a certain way, their anticipation: *"Veni, Domine Iesu!"* (*Rev* 22:20).

In the humble signs of bread and wine, changed into his body and blood, Christ walks beside us as our strength and our food for the journey, and he enables us to become, for everyone, witnesses of hope. If, in the presence of this mystery, reason experiences its limits, the heart, enlightened by the grace of the Holy Spirit, clearly sees the response that is demanded, and bows low in adoration and unbounded love.

Let us make our own the words of Saint Thomas Aquinas, an eminent theologian and an impassioned poet of Christ in the Eucharist, and turn in hope to the contemplation of that goal to which our hearts aspire in their thirst for joy and peace:

> *Bone pastor, panis vere,*
> *Iesu, nostri miserere …*
> *Come then, good Shepherd, bread divine,*
> *Still show to us thy mercy sign;*
> *Oh, feed us, still keep us thine;*
> *So we may see thy glories shine*
> *in fields of immortality.*
> *O thou, the wisest, mightiest, best,*
> *Our present food, our future rest,*
> *Come, make us each thy chosen guest,*
> *Co-heirs of thine, and comrades blest*
> *With saints whose dwelling is with thee.*

Given in Rome, at Saint Peter's, on 17 April, Holy Thursday, in the year 2003, the Twenty-fifth of my Pontificate, the Year of the Rosary.

IOANNES PAULUS II

NOTES

1   Second Vatican Ecumenical Council, Dogmatic Constitution on the Church, *Lumen Gentium*, 11.

2   Second Vatican Ecumenical Council, Decree on the Ministry and Life of Priests, *Presbyterorum Ordinis*, 5.

3   Cf. John Paul II, Apostolic Letter *Rosarium Virginis Mariae* (16 October 2002), 21: AAS 95 (2003), 19.

4   This is the title which I gave to an autobiographical testimony issued for my fiftieth anniversary of priestly ordination.

5   *Leonis XIII P.M. Acta*, XXII (1903), 115-136.

6   AAS 39 (1947), 521-595.

7   AAS 57 (1965), 753-774.

8   AAS 72 (1980), 113-148.

9   Cf. Second Vatican Ecumenical Council, Constitution *Sacrosanctum Concilium*, 47: " ... our Savior instituted the eucharistic sacrifice of his body and blood, in order to perpetuate the sacrifice of the cross throughout time, until he should return."

10   *Catechism of the Catholic Church*, 1085.

11   Second Vatican Ecumenical Council, Dogmatic Constitution on the Church, *Lumen Gentium*, 3.

12   Cf. Paul VI, *Solemn Profession of Faith* (30 June 1968), 24: AAS 60 (1968), 442; John Paul II, Apostolic Letter *Dominicae Cenae* (24 February 1980), 12: AAS 72 (1980), 142.

13   *Catechism of the Catholic Church*, 1382.

14   *Catechism of the Catholic Church*, 1367.

15   *In Epistolam ad Hebraeos Homiliae, Hom.* 17,3: PG 63, 131.

16   Cf. Ecumenical Council of Trent, Session XXII, *Doctrina de ss. Missae Sacrificio*, Chapter 2: DS 1743: "It is one and the same victim here offering himself by the ministry of his priests, who then offered himself on the cross; it is only the manner of offering that is different."

17   Pius XII, Encyclical Letter *Mediator Dei* (20 November 1947): AAS 39 (1947), 548.

18   John Paul II, Encyclical Letter *Redemptor Hominis* (15 March 1979), 20: AAS 71 (1979), 310.

19   Dogmatic Constitution on the Church, *Lumen Gentium*, 11.

20   *De Sacramentis*, V, 4, 26: CSEL 73, 70.

21   *In Ioannis Evangelium*, XII, 20: PG 74, 726.

22   Encyclical Letter *Mysterium Fidei* (3 September 1965): AAS 57 (1965), 764.

23   Session XIII, *Decretum de ss. Eucharistia*, Chapter 4: DS 1642.

24   *Mystagogical Catecheses*, IV, 6: SCh 126, 138.

25   Second Vatican Ecumenical Council, Dogmatic Constitution on Divine Revelation, *Dei Verbum*, 8.

26   *Solemn Profession of Faith* (30 June 1968), 25: AAS 60 (1968), 442-443.

27   *Sermo IV in Hebdomadam Sanctam*: CSCO 413/Syr. 182, 55.

28   Anaphora.

29   Eucharistic Prayer III.

30   Solemnity of the Body and Blood of Christ, Second Vespers, Antiphon to the *Magnificat*.

31   *Missale Romanum*, Embolism following the Lord's Prayer.

32   *Ad Ephesios*, 20: PG 5, 661.

33   Cf. Second Vatican Ecumenical Council, Pastoral Constitution on the Church in the Modern World, *Gaudium et Spes*, 39.

34   "Do you wish to honor the body of Christ? Do not ignore him when he is naked. Do not pay him homage in the temple clad in silk, only then to neglect him outside where he is cold and ill-clad. He who said: 'This is my body' is the same who said: 'You saw me hungry and you gave me no food,' and 'Whatever you did to the least of my brothers you did also to me' ... What good is it if the eucharistic table is overloaded with golden chalices when your brother is dying of hunger. Start by satisfying his hunger and then with what is left you may adorn the altar as well": Saint John Chrysostom, *In Evangelium S. Matthaei, hom.* 50:3-4: PG 58, 508-509; cf. John Paul II, Encyclical Letter *Sollicitudo Rei Socialis* (30 December 1987), 31: AAS 80 (1988), 553-556.

35   Dogmatic Constitution *Lumen Gentium*, 3.

36   Ibid.

37   Second Vatican Ecumenical Council, Decree on the Missionary Activity of the Church, *Ad Gentes*, 5.

38   "Moses took the blood and threw it upon the people, and said: 'Behold the blood of the Covenant which the Lord has made with you in accordance with all these words'" (*Ex* 24:8).

39   Cf. Second Vatican Ecumenical Council, Dogmatic Constitution on the Church, *Lumen Gentium*, 1.

40   Cf. ibid., 9.

41   Cf. Second Vatican Ecumenical Council, Decree on the Life and Ministry of Priests, *Presbyterorum Ordinis*, 5. The same Decree, in No. 6, says: "No Christian community can be built up which does not grow from and hinge on the celebration of the most holy Eucharist."

42   *In Epistolam I ad Corinthios Homiliae*, 24, 2: PG 61, 200; Cf. Didache, IX, 4: F.X. Funk, I, 22; Saint Cyprian, Ep. LXIII, 13: PL 4, 384.

43   PO 26, 206.

44   Second Vatican Ecumenical Council, Dogmatic Constitution on the Church, *Lumen Gentium*, 1.

45   Cf. Ecumenical Council of Trent, Session XIII, *Decretum de ss. Eucharistia*, Canon 4: DS 1654.

46   Cf. *Rituale Romanum: De sacra communione et de cultu mysterii eucharistici extra Missam*, 36 (No. 80).

47   Cf. ibid., 38-39 (Nos. 86-90).

48   John Paul II, Apostolic Letter *Novo Millennio Ineunte* (6 January 2001), 32: AAS 93 (2001), 288.

49   "In the course of the day the faithful should not omit visiting the Blessed Sacrament, which in accordance with liturgical law must be reserved in churches with great reverence in a prominent place. Such visits are a sign of gratitude, an expression of love and an acknowledgment of the Lord's presence": Paul VI, Encyclical Letter *Mysterium Fidei* (3 September 1965): AAS 57 (1965), 771.

50 *Visite al SS. Sacramento e a Maria Santissima*, Introduction: *Opere Ascetiche*, Avellino, 2000, 295.

51 No. 857.

52 Ibid.

53 Ibid.

54 Cf. Congregation for the Doctrine of the Faith, Letter *Sacerdotium Ministeriale* (6 August 1983), III.2: AAS 75 (1983), 1005.

55 Second Vatican Ecumenical Council, Dogmatic Constitution on the Church, *Lumen Gentium*, 10.

56 Ibid.

57 Cf. *Institutio Generalis:* Editio typica tertia, No. 147.

58 Cf. Dogmatic Constitution on the Church, *Lumen Gentium*, 10 and 28; Decree on the Ministry and Life of Priests, *Presbyterorum Ordinis*, 2.

59 "The minister of the altar acts in the person of Christ inasmuch as he is head, making an offering in the name of all the members": Pius XII, Encyclical Letter *Mediator Dei* (20 November 1947): AAS 39 (1947), 556; cf. Pius X, Apostolic Exhortation *Haerent Animo* (4 August 1908): *Acta Pii X*, IV, 16; Pius XI, Encyclical Letter *Ad Catholici Sacerdotii* (20 December 1935): AAS 28 (1936), 20.

60 Apostolic Letter *Dominicae Cenae* (24 February 1980), 8: AAS 72 (1980), 128-129.

61 Congregation for the Doctrine of the Faith, Letter *Sacerdotium Ministeriale* (6 August 1983), III.4: AAS 75 (1983), 1006; cf. Fourth Lateran Ecumenical Council, Chapter 1, Constitution on the Catholic Faith, *Firmiter Credimus:* DS 802.

62 Second Vatican Ecumenical Council, Decree on Ecumenism, *Unitatis Redintegratio*, 22.

63 Apostolic Letter *Dominicae Cenae* (24 February 1980), 2: AAS 72 (1980), 115.

64 Decree on the Life and Ministry of Priests *Presbyterorum Ordinis*, 14.

65 Ibid., 13; cf. *Code of Canon Law*, Canon 904; *Code of Canons of the Eastern Churches*, Canon 378.

66 Decree on the Ministry and Life of Priests, *Presbytero-rum Ordinis*, 6.

67 Cf. Final Report, II.C.1: *L' Osservatore Romano* (10 December 1985), 7.

68 Second Vatican Ecumenical Council, Dogmatic Constitution on the Church, *Lumen Gentium*, 26.

69 Nicolas Cabasilas, *Life in Christ*, IV, 10: SCh 355, 270.

70 *Camino de Perfección*, Chapter 35.

71 Cf. Congregation for the Doctrine of the Faith, Letter to the Bishops of the Catholic Church on Some Aspects of the Church Understood as Communion, *Communionis Notio* (28 May 1992), 4: AAS 85 (1993), 839-840.

72 Cf. Second Vatican Ecumenical Council, Dogmatic Constitution on the Church, *Lumen Gentium*, 14.

73 *Homiliae in Isaiam*,6, 3: PG 56, 139.

74 No. 1385; cf. *Code of Canon Law*, Canon 916; *Code of Canons of the Eastern Churches*, Canon 711.

75 Address to the Members of the Sacred Apostolic Penitentiary and the Penitentiaries of the Patriarchal Basilicas of Rome (30 January 1981): AAS 73 (1981), 203. Cf. Ecumenical Council of Trent, Sess. XIII, *Decretum de ss. Eucharistia*, Chapter 7 and Canon 11: DS 1647, 1661.

76 Canon 915; *Code of Canons of the Eastern Churches*, Canon 712.

77 Dogmatic Constitution on the Church, *Lumen Gentium*, 14.

78 Saint Thomas Aquinas, *Summa Theologiae*, III, q. 73, a. 3c.

79 Congregation for the Doctrine of the Faith, Letter to the Bishops of the Catholic Church on Some Aspects of the Church Understood as Communion, *Communionis Notio* (28 May 1992), 11: AAS 85 (1993), 844.

80 Cf. Second Vatican Ecumenical Council, Dogmatic Constitution on the Church, *Lumen Gentium*, 23.

81 *Ad Smyrnaeos*, 8: PG 5, 713.

82 Second Vatican Ecumenical Council, Dogmatic Constitution on the Church, *Lumen Gentium*, 23.

83 Congregation for the Doctrine of the Faith, Letter to the Bishops of the Catholic Church on Some Aspects of the Church Understood as Communion, *Communionis Notio* (28 May 1992), 14: AAS 85 (1993), 847.

84 *Sermo* 272: PL 38, 1247.

85 Ibid., 1248.

86 Cf. Nos. 31-51: AAS 90 (1998), 731-746.

87 Cf. ibid., Nos. 48-49: AAS 90 (1998), 744.

88 No. 36: AAS 93 (2001), 291-292.

89 Cf. Decree on Ecumenism *Unitatis Redintegratio*, 1.

90 Cf. Dogmatic Constitution on the Church, *Lumen Gentium*, 11.

91 "Join all of us, who share the one bread and the one cup, to one another in the communion of the one Holy Spirit": *Anaphora of the Liturgy of Saint Basil*.

92 Cf. *Code of Canon Law*, Canon 908; *Code of Canons of the Eastern Churches*, Canon 702; Pontifical Council for the Promotion of Christian Unity, *Ecumenical Directory*, 25 March 1993, 122-125, 129-131: AAS 85 (1993), 1086-1089; Congregation for the Doctrine of the Faith, Letter *Ad Exsequendam* (18 May 2001): AAS 93 (2001), 786.

93 "Divine law forbids any common worship which would damage the unity of the Church, or involve formal acceptance of falsehood or the danger of deviation in the faith, of scandal, or of indifferentism": Decree on the Eastern Catholic Churches, *Orientalium Ecclesiarum*, 26.

94 No. 45: AAS 87 (1995), 948.

95 Decree on the Eastern Catholic Churches, *Orientalium Ecclesiarum*, 27.

96 Cf. *Code of Canon Law*, Canon 844 §§ 3-4; *Code of Canons of the Eastern Churches*, Canon 671 §§ 3-4.

97 No. 46: AAS 87 (1995), 948.

98 Cf. Second Vatican Ecumenical Council, Decree on Ecumenism, *Unitatis Redintegratio*, 22.

99 *Code of Canon Law*, Canon 844; *Code of Canons of the Eastern Churches*, Canon 671.

100 Cf. AAS 91 (1999), 1155-1172.

101 No. 22: AAS 92 (2000), 485.

102 Cf. No. 21: AAS 95 (2003), 20.

103 No. 29: AAS 93 (2001), 285.

104 Saint Thomas Aquinas, *Summa Theologiae*, III, q. 83, a. 4c.

Good News:
L'Osservatore Romano

Good news seldom makes headlines. It is remarkable, therefore, that the official Vatican newspaper, *L'Osservatore Romano* (the Roman Observer), has been serving the cause of the gospel and the Holy See for more than 142 years. Remarkable because every daily headline it puts forth is a proclamation of the "Good News" as it is embodied in the person of the Pope and the dynamism of the Church.

Ironically, *L'Osservatore Romano* was born in circumstances of very bad news in 1861 during the upheaval of late nineteenth-century Italian politics. Catholic intellectuals, gathered in Rome, founded what would eventually become the Vatican newspaper we have come to know. That both the papacy and *L'Osservatore Romano* survive today with even greater esteem and authority attests that the pen is truly mightier than the sword.

"Since the Lord called me to the Chair of Peter," Pope John Paul II has said, "I myself have not ceased to follow, day by day, the religious, pastoral, cultural, political and social progress of the newspaper." More than just a reader, the Pope, better than any of his predecessors, has used *L'Osservatore Romano* to aid his mission as pontiff. As the photographs in this book clearly illustrate, the Holy Father puts his words into action and *L'Osservatore Romano* photography records those moments that reflect the Pope in the core of his essence as a disciple of Christ.

Pope John Paul II is the first pope to compile a complete visual record of his pontificate. Aiding the Holy Father in this visual proclamation of the Gospel are *L'Osservatore Romano's* two primary photographers. Arturo Mari and Francesco Sforza daily take their turns "shadowing" the Pope, unobtrusively focusing their cameras on John Paul's witness to the Gospels. Their close proximity to the pontiff makes these men not only recorders of history but history makers themselves. Case in point: May 13, 1981. Francesco, photographing the Wednesday general audience in St. Peter's Square, was with the Pope in the jeep that wound its way through the immense crowd. Before his camera—before his eyes—the Pope was struck down by Ali Acga's bullets. Confusion reigned; Francesco felt compelled as a photographer to continue capturing these historic yet tragic moments on film. But as a man—as a Christian—he was also compelled to put his camera aside and give aid to the wounded pope, which he ultimately did. At that moment, Francesco lived the words of Pope John XXIII who said *L'Osservatore Romano* safeguards "the honesty and honor of the human condition and dignity." Every photograph Francesco and Arturo shoot reflects this integrity.

Today, as the Church "puts out into the deep," *L'Osservatore Romano* uses the latest publishing technologies in its efforts to aid the New Evangelization. Additionally, the paper is also published in seven language editions, including English. Regardless of what the headline may actually say on any given edition, *L'Osservatore Romano's* message is always constant, always clear: "The Kingdom of God is in your midst." This is good news indeed.

ARTURO MARI (top) and FRANCESCO SFORZA are *L' Osservatore Romano's* principal photographers.

WE ARE NOT BORN TO KEEP A MUSEUM,
BUT RATHER TO CULTIVATE A LIVING GARDEN.

Pope John XXIII (1958-1963)

EVANGELIZATION, ABOVE ALL!
OUR AGE IS NOT A TIME FOR MERELY PRESERVING
WHAT EXISTS BUT FOR MISSION!

Pope John Paul II (October 11, 2000, L'Osservatore Romano)

Both Blessed Pope John XXIII and Pope John Paul II proclaim the wisdom that has guided the Pope John Paul II Cultural Center from its beginning: bringing the Gospel to life in ever-new ways by means of a living dialogue between faith and culture.

At the center of the logo is the cross of Jesus Christ, a Greek Cross with arms of equal length extending beyond the boundaries of the square, thus symbolizing the Christian faith transcending all human boundaries.

The cross separates the logo into four quadrants with the upper left and lower right quadrants symbolically representing the Keys of St. Peter, symbol of the Papacy; since what Peter and his successors bind on earth is also bound in heaven, one key is placed higher than the other in the logo. In the lower left quadrant, a wave represents the waters of Baptism, the life-giving waters of faith. At the upper right quadrant, a leaf represents growth, a reminder that the tiny mustard seed can become the mightiest of trees.

Where the arms of the cross intersect, a white square reminds us of the mystery of Jesus Christ, the Redeemer of Man, center of the universe and human history. As we are drawn to that openness, we enter into the mystery of God; then and there, we begin to hear the Good News in a more profound way and are empowered to proclaim it by our very lives.

The museum experience at the Pope John Paul II Cultural Center helps individuals, families and groups examine the role of faith in formulating and sustaining the values of our culture through a number of interrelated facilities. These include a state-of-the-art interactive gallery experience designed for people of all ages, works of art from the Vatican Museums and other collections, and exhibits and film on the life and teachings of Pope John Paul II and the history of the papacy. The Intercultural Forum for Studies in Faith and Culture is a center for scholarly research and dialogue on the issues most central to the pontificate of John Paul II.

"A Christian will joyously collaborate in promoting true culture because he knows that the Good News of Christ reinforces in man the spiritual values that are at the heart of every culture in every historical period." Pope John Paul II.

LORD,
MAY WE ALWAYS BE DRAWN TO
THIS ALTAR OF SACRIFICE.
UNITED IN FAITH AND LOVE,
MAY WE BE NOURISHED BY
THE BODY OF CHRIST AND TRANSFORMED
INTO HIS LIKENESS, WHO LIVES AND
REIGNS WITH YOU AND THE HOLY SPIRIT,
ONE GOD FOR EVER AND EVER.

Prayer after Communion, Rite of Dedication of an Altar